COME AND SEE

COME AND SEE

An Invitation to a Radical Encounter With Jesus

Shannon T. L. Kearns

HODDER FAITH
YOUNG EXPLORERS

First published in Great Britain in 2025 by
Hodder Faith Young Explorers
An imprint of John Murray (Publishers)

1

A CIP catalogue record for this title is available from the British Library

Hardback ISBN 978 1 399 81815 5
ebook ISBN 978 1 399 81816 2

Typeset in Avenir LT by Hewer Text UK Ltd, Edinburgh
Printed and bound in Great Britain by Clays Ltd, Elcograf S.p.A.

John Murray policy is to use papers that are natural, renewable and recyclable products and made from wood grown in sustainable forests. The logging and manufacturing processes are expected to conform to the environmental regulations of the country of origin.

Carmelite House
50 Victoria Embankment
London EC4Y 0DZ

www.hodderfaithyoungexplorers.co.uk

John Murray Press, part of Hodder & Stoughton Limited
An Hachette UK company

The authorised representative in the EEA is Hachette Ireland,
8 Castlecourt Centre, Dublin 15, D15 XTP3, Ireland (email: info@hbgi.ie)

CONTENTS

ACKNOWLEDGMENTS

There are so many people who taught me to read and love the Bible. Here are some folks who have been influential: Fr. Daniel Berrigan, Rob Bell, Ched Myers, Dorothy Day, Joy Ladin, Jaques Ellul, and all of my professors at Union Theological Seminary in New York.

To my wife, Ashley Hovell, for always supporting me and cheering me on. I love the life we continue to build together.

To the incredible team at Hodder Faith for championing this book and making it beautiful.

To Trinity McFadden and the Bindery team for all of your support and work to bring much needed books to the world.

To my friends and co-conspirators Adam, Brian, Kim, and Stephanie. Your love and support keeps me going.

LETTER TO THE READER

Hello and welcome!

I'm so glad that you're here and ready to dive in! Welcome to *Come and See*!

Whether you've read and heard stuff about the Bible a lot OR you're totally new to the Bible, you are welcome here. If you're feeling overwhelmed by how to read and understand the Bible, this book will give you some insights and tools to help you along the way.

Even more important than learning to read and understand the Bible is figuring out how to connect it to your life. What does it mean to live out your faith, here and now? How can these ancient stories still speak to your life today? Answering those questions can sometimes be tricky. That's why this devotional goes beyond just reading the stories, it invites you to take the stories and connect them to your heart and your hands.

For every story, there are ways to connect it to your own life, and even some ideas to try some things out to put your faith into motion. Our faith isn't meant to be just in our heads, it's meant to be in our hearts and in our hands, and lived out every single day.

So I hope this devotional can be like Jesus' invitation to some of his first followers to "come and see" what the life of discipleship looks like. To come and see what it feels like to follow Jesus. To come and see what living out your faith here and now is like.

The invitation is offered, now it's up to you.

INTRODUCTION TO THE BOOK

HOW TO USE THIS BOOK

Each day's entry is broken up into four sections. First you read the text, then you reflect, then connect your head and your heart, then connect your heart and your hands. You can read one entry every day or spend a couple days on each entry. I often find that by reading the same stories several times I see new things in them each time! You could spend an entire week on just one entry.

Here's a bit about what each of the sections mean:

> READ

For each entry there is a Bible passage to read. When you can, or have extra time, it can be good to read the verses around the passage because the whole story matters and we'll learn even more when we understand the fuller picture. Spend some time reading through the story. You might underline things that jump out at you, put a question mark by things you have questions about, or take notes on things you want to remember.

> REFLECT

After each passage there is a reflection written to help you understand the story in a new way, to provide you with some context or history you might need to understand it better, or to spark some new ways to understand it. There are lots of different ways to read and understand a lot of these stories, so this reflection is just one way. Don't worry if you saw something different in the story! That doesn't mean you read it wrong, it just means you saw something different. Sometimes those places of difference can reveal a lot. Use the reflection to open you up to new ways of seeing.

> CONNECT HEAD AND HEART

In this section you'll find some questions to inspire you to go deeper. These questions will ask you to reflect on the story and to think about how it relates to your own life. These questions will support you in making deeper connections. They will help you to explore where you might have similar feelings to the people in the story or where your feelings and experiences are totally different. You can use these prompts to write out your thoughts in a paper journal, in a doc on your phone or computer, or something else entirely! Do what works for you.

You could also use these prompts as discussion starters: maybe you're going through this devotional with a friend, a youth group, or with a family member, and these questions could inspire a conversation.

> CONNECT HEART AND HANDS

The last section are adventures to get you out of your head and into your body. Your faith is a practice. It's something you do. These items encourage you to try some experiments and see how they resonate. For some of the experiments, you might need to take a parent or guardian along, or invite an older friend. You might make something, or make a plan for something bigger than you can do right now. These adventures might challenge you to change something or push you out of your comfort zone. It's worth trying these things as part of the invitation to "come and see" what following Jesus can really look and feel like. Your faith isn't just something you believe or carry in your heart, it impacts the way you live your life. What an exciting thing!

THE LOOP

These steps aren't linear, meaning you don't just go through them and then you're done. It's better to think of them as a loop: you go through them in order, and then it takes you back to the beginning. After you've done your adventures, it might cause you to read the story in a completely new way. Or maybe you'll have more to journal about or to talk about with a friend. Going back and doing the steps again will help you to take your reflections even deeper and to incorporate bigger changes you might want to make in your faith practice and life.

WHAT IF I MESS UP?

Don't worry if you miss a day (or three!), just pick up where you left off. This isn't about perfection, it's about creating a practice to nourish and nurture your faith and connect it to your daily life.

INTRODUCTION TO THE BIBLE

Before we jump into our devotional, it's helpful if we have a working understanding of the Bible. It's easy to think of the Bible as a book. After all, we call it a book, it's bound like a book, we can buy it in stores as a single volume. It's better, however, to understand the Bible as a library of books. It's a collection of a variety of different types of texts: histories, stories, letters, poetry, the list goes on.

We can think of the Bible as a record of people who are trying to make sense of some really big questions: Who are we? Why are we here? What are we here to do? How did things get the way they are? Why do bad things happen? What is our relationship supposed to be with ourselves, with other people, and with God/the Divine?

Each one of these books is written by a particular person (or sometimes groups of people), in a particular time, in a particular place.

All these things impact the way they tell the stories, as do the outside forces (like politics, other religious practices of people around them, and historical events) they are responding to. All of that together shapes the point they are trying to make (and often how the original receivers would have understood it).

Many of the books of the Bible started as an oral tradition; spoken stories and histories that were passed down through generations before finally being written down. And when they were originally written down, there were no chapters and verse numbers! Those were added later to make it easier to read. But that's why it's so important that we don't just memorize verses or read things outside of their whole context; these stories weren't meant to be read that way. They were meant to tell a whole story. While some verses might be comforting, taking them out of their surroundings might make them mean something they weren't meant to.

The Bible is broken into two parts and consists of sixty-six books (though the Catholic Church has seven other books that they consider part of their Scriptures). Some people call these parts the Old Testament and the New Testament, but a better way to describe them would be the Hebrew Scriptures and the Christian Scriptures. Each of these parts of the Bible has its own history, its own challenges of interpretation, and its own process of getting put together.

Why does all of this matter? Because this complicated library of books has been used for both really amazing things and really damaging things. It's been misunderstood and misused. It's been used as a weapon, but also as a comfort. It's been called holy and profane. It's been said to be both the most important book of all and completely outdated.

As we enter into this adventure, we want to read the Bible as it is, in all its complexity. We want to understand what type of book we're reading and a bit about why it was written and who it was written for (and how they would have understood it). We want to bring all of our intelligence with us as we engage with stories that can encourage, challenge, and deepen our faith.

We don't have to be afraid to ask questions, to wrestle, to use all of our wisdom in trying to understand this library. In fact, grappling with the Bible is one of the most faithful things we can do.

INTRODUCTION TO THE HEBREW SCRIPTURES

The Hebrew Scriptures (often called the Old Testament) is made up of a bunch of different types of books: histories, poetry, philosophy, books of law, books written telling the stories of leaders and battles, and more!

Some of the books in the Hebrew Scriptures were written in response to other books, which means we sometimes have stories or teachings that contradict each other, or that are in conversation with one another. This can sometimes make it complicated to understand what to believe or who is "right," which is why it's so important that as we read, we listen to smart people who can help us understand these stories (and when and where they were written) better. For instance, there is a story in the book of Nehemiah about God commanding the people to cast out everyone who was a foreigner. At the same time, the book of Ruth was written, which is all about how a woman who was a foreigner refused to leave her mother-in-law and joined the people of Israel. (She even becomes part of the family that Jesus is born into!)

A lot of the Hebrew Scriptures are written in the context of exile, which means a time when the people of Israel were away from their homeland and under the rule of another nation. Because of that context, the books are often about how to preserve their identity in the midst of exile. They were asking BIG questions: What are the things that set them apart from the other nations? Why do bad things keep happening to them? Where is God in the midst of the bad things? How can they do better? These are big questions, and questions you might be wrestling with today! Which is why it's so beautiful that we have these records of people many, many, many years ago asking the same types of questions.

Jesus and his followers would have known the Hebrew Scriptures.

Jesus and his followers would have known the Hebrew Scriptures. They would have grown up hearing these stories, praying these prayers, and being taught through them how God shows up in the world and in their community. These texts were the foundation of their religious tradition and deeply influenced the stories Jesus told and the mission he lived out. Understanding these stories and how they informed Jesus' thinking and beliefs can help to better inform our own faith today.

We, too, are invited to "come and see" how we fit into the story of God and how these stories can still speak to us today.

STARTING WITH GOODNESS

Genesis 1:26–31

READ

Then God said, "Let us make humanity in our image to resemble us so that they may take charge of the fish of the sea, the birds in the sky, the livestock, all the earth, and all the crawling things on earth." God created humanity in God's own image, in the divine image God created them, male and female God created them.

God blessed them and said to them, "Be fertile and multiply; fill the earth and master it. Take charge of the fish of the sea, the birds in the sky, and everything crawling on the ground." Then God said, "I now give to you all the plants on the earth that yield seeds and all the trees whose fruit produces its seeds within it. These will be your food. To all wildlife, to all the birds in the sky, and to everything crawling on the ground—to everything that breathes—I give all the green grasses for food." And that's what happened. God saw everything he had made: it was supremely good.

There was evening and there was morning: the sixth day.

REFLECT

The very first book of the Hebrew Scriptures starts off with a story. A story where God brings everything into being simply by speaking. It's a story of an ordered world: six days of creation, and then a day of rest.

These early stories in the Bible came from a culture of storytellers, people who would pass them on orally before they were eventually written down. These stories were told to help people make sense of who they are, where they came from, and why things are the way they are.

The story of creation starts with goodness. After each day of creation, God looks at the work they've done and "God saw how good it was." And then, after the sixth day and the creation of human beings, God looks around at all of it and says "it was supremely good." Creation is good.

The storytellers say God's original plan for creation is harmony and goodness.

In this beginning story there is harmony between creatures. There is an order. Everyone has what they need. People are given certain kinds of plants and fruit to eat; for the animals, other things to eat. Everyone had responsibilities to the tending of things. Everyone had their own role to play. There wasn't competition or fighting, there was co-operation.

The storytellers say God's original plan for creation is harmony and goodness.

It's easy sometimes to focus on things that aren't great in the world, to get caught up in the violence or selfishness, or to think about how we mess up, but this creation story reminds us that we are rooted in goodness. In the beginning everything was supremely good. Starting with that message roots us in hope. We can get back to that goodness. In fact, that is what God wants for us, to be back to a place of harmony where everything and everyone are working together.

CONNECT HEAD AND HEART

- **Why do you think the storytellers of Genesis started with this creation story?**
- **What does it mean to you to be created in the image of God?**
- **What does this story of a world in total harmony make you feel?**
- **What other stories have you heard about the beginning of the world?**
- **What other stories have you heard about the creation of human beings?**
- **What do the differences in the stories you may have heard and these stories make you think about?**

To start that work, we need to remember our own goodness; that we are created in the image of God and that we have a role to play in the order of things. When we start rooted in our goodness, it changes how we move through the world.

When we remember our own goodness, we can also remember to look at other people as good too. They are also created and rooted in goodness. They, too, have a special role to play. When we focus on that we are better able to work together.

CONNECT HEART AND HANDS

- **Learn more about the plants and trees that grow where you live. What is the climate of your area best suited for? What is currently in season?**
- **Ask a trusted adult in your life to help you cook a meal entirely from local and in-season ingredients. After you're done, reflect on what the experience was like.**
- **Put a note on your mirror or in a place where you'll see it every day that says, "You are VERY GOOD." How does reading that shift your mood and how you feel about yourself?**

We can also extend that view out from humans to think about the animals and plants. Remembering the goal to live in harmony with all created things, we can think about how to care for the environment and live in harmony with that as well. We can pay attention to the impact we're having on creation and try to be good stewards of it.

Let's remember that we are created good and work to see the goodness in everyone and everything we meet.

WRESTLING WITH GOD

Genesis 32

READ

Jacob went on his way, and God's messengers approached him. When Jacob saw them, he said, "This is God's camp," and he named that sacred place Mahanaim. Jacob sent messengers ahead of him to his brother Esau, toward the land of Seir, the open country of Edom. He gave them these orders: "Say this to my master Esau. This is the message of your servant Jacob: 'I've lived as an immigrant with Laban, where I've stayed till now. I own cattle, donkeys, flocks, men servants, and women servants. I'm sending this message to my master now to ask that he be kind.'"

The messengers returned to Jacob and said, "We went out to your brother Esau, and he's coming to meet you with four hundred men."

Jacob was terrified and felt trapped, so he divided the people with him, and the flocks, cattle, and camels, into two camps. He thought, If Esau meets the first camp and attacks it, at least one camp will be left to escape.

Jacob said, "Lord, God of my father Abraham, God of my father Isaac, who said to me, 'Go back to your country and your relatives, and I'll make sure things go well for you,' I don't deserve how loyal and truthful you've been to your servant. I went away across the Jordan with just my staff, but now I've become two camps. Save me from my brother Esau! I'm afraid he will come and kill me, the mothers, and their children. You were the one who told me, 'I will make sure things go well for you, and I will make your descendants like the sand of the sea, so many you won't be able to count them.'"

CONNECT HEAD AND HEART

> How do you think Jacob felt when he heard Esau wanted to see him?

> How do you think Esau felt about seeing his brother again after so long?

> Have you ever gotten something you wanted, but it came with something you didn't want (like Jacob getting a blessing AND a limp)? What happened? What did you learn from that situation?

> What do you think it would be like to demand a blessing from the Divine? What kind of blessing do you hope you'd get?

> If God was going to give you a new name to represent a new identity, what do you think that name would be?

Jacob spent that night there. From what he had acquired, he set aside a gift for his brother Esau: two hundred female goats and twenty male goats, two hundred ewes and twenty rams, thirty nursing camels with their young, forty cows and ten bulls, and twenty female donkeys and ten male donkeys. He separated these herds and gave them to his servants. He said to them, "Go ahead of me and put some distance between each of the herds." He ordered the first group, "When my brother Esau meets you and asks you, 'Who are you with? Where are you going? And whose herds are these in front of you?' say, 'They are your servant Jacob's, a gift sent to my master Esau. And Jacob is actually right behind us.'" He also ordered the second group, the third group, and everybody following the herds, "Say exactly the same thing to Esau when you find him. Say also, 'Your servant Jacob is right behind us.'" Jacob thought, I may be able to pacify Esau with the gift I'm sending ahead. When I meet him, perhaps he will be kind to me. So Jacob sent the gift ahead of him, but he spent that night in the camp.

Many of us have experiences in our lives that teach us something, but also change us.

Jacob got up during the night, took his two wives, his two women servants, and his eleven sons, and crossed the Jabbok River's shallow water. He took them and everything that belonged to him, and he helped them cross the river. But Jacob stayed apart by himself, and a man wrestled with him until dawn broke. When the man saw that he couldn't defeat Jacob, he grabbed Jacob's thigh and tore a muscle in Jacob's thigh as he wrestled with him. The man said, "Let me go because the dawn is breaking."

But Jacob said, "I won't let you go until you bless me."

He said to Jacob, "What's your name?" and he said, "Jacob." Then he said, "Your name won't be Jacob any longer, but Israel, because you struggled with God and with men and won."

Jacob also asked and said, "Tell me your name."

But he said, "Why do you ask for my name?" and he blessed Jacob there. Jacob named the place Peniel, "because I've seen God face-to-face, and my life has been saved." The sun rose as Jacob passed Penuel, limping because of his thigh. Therefore, Israelites don't eat the tendon attached to the thigh muscle to this day, because he grabbed Jacob's thigh muscle at the tendon.

REFLECT

Our story today is actually part of a much longer story going back several chapters, so let's spend a little bit of time catching up first! Jacob and Esau are twin brothers, but they are very, very different from one another. Jacob likes to stay at home, helping out in the kitchen, while Esau likes to hunt and be outdoors. Because of this, their father favors Esau over Jacob.

When the two of them were younger, their father, Isaac, was close to death. He was losing his sight. He wanted to offer the traditional blessing to the oldest son before he died. While Esau was out hunting, their mother helped Jacob to disguise himself as Esau so he could trick his father and get the blessing. When Esau found out what Jacob had done, he was furious and so Jacob ran away from home.

As Jacob travels with his wives and children and all of his livestock, looking for a new place to settle, word comes to him that Esau wants to see him. They haven't seen each other for many years and Jacob is really worried that Esau is still angry and wants to do harm to him. And that's where our story picks up today.

Jacob is a smart guy. He's crafty and tricky. He's used to finding ways to get out of hard situations. So he tries to figure out how he can endure this encounter with his brother and not lose everything he's gained in the years they've been apart.

He separates his family and livestock into several different groups. He's trying to be less threatening to Esau, but also trying to protect his property so that if Esau intends to do him violence he won't lose everything. It's a calculated move.

In the midst of all of this scheming, on the night before he's supposed to see his brother again after many years apart, Jacob spends time completely alone. And in the night, a man comes to him and they wrestle. It's kind of a strange part of the story.

Some scholars say that this man is an angel. Others say it's God. Clearly something profound and holy is happening in the darkness of the night. Jacob is wrestling. Struggling. Refusing to let go.

As the night wears on, the man injures Jacob and then tells him to let go. Jacob, ever looking out for what he can get out of a situation, says, "I won't let you go until you bless me."

Finally, the man blesses Jacob AND gives him a new name, calling him Israel.

Jacob names this now sacred site, marking it as the place where he met God. And he goes away from this encounter limping.

It's kind of a wild story and it's sandwiched in this encounter of Jacob seeing his brother again. But there's something powerful here. A man who is used to getting what he wants DOES get his blessing, but he also gets injured and has to walk with a limp.

CONNECT HEART AND HANDS

- Spend some time in silence and then write out the blessing you'd like to receive from God. Put it somewhere either where you can see it often, or where it feels safe and you can look at it when you need to.
- Think about someone you might need to apologize to. What's something you can do to make amends to that person?
- Find a list of baby names and their meanings in a book or online. Pick out a new name that has a meaning and qualities you aspire to.

Many of us have experiences in our lives that teach us something, but also change us. Maybe it's experiencing the death of someone you love, or your parents divorcing. Maybe you lose a friend or move to a new community. Maybe you try something and fail OR you try something and succeed! You are changed by what you went through. Maybe you don't walk with a limp, but you're not the same person you were before the experience.

In the Bible when people have experiences like this, they are often given new names to mark the change in them and to show the community that they've changed.

What I love about this story is Jacob's willingness to hold on for his blessing. To know that the blessing is worth what it might cost him, because he was being changed into something new.

May we all have the courage to hold on for the blessing.

MOSES GETS CALLED

Exodus 3:1–16

READ

Moses was taking care of the flock for his father-in-law Jethro, Midian's priest. He led his flock out to the edge of the desert, and he came to God's mountain called Horeb. The LORD's messenger appeared to him in a flame of fire in the middle of a bush. Moses saw that the bush was in flames, but it didn't burn up. Then Moses said to himself, Let me check out this amazing sight and find out why the bush isn't burning up.

When the LORD saw that he was coming to look, God called to him out of the bush, "Moses, Moses!"

Moses said, "I'm here."

Then the LORD said, "Don't come any closer! Take off your sandals, because you are standing on holy ground." He continued, "I am the God of your father, Abraham's God, Isaac's God, and Jacob's God." Moses hid his face because he was afraid to look at God.

Then the LORD said, "I've clearly seen my people oppressed in Egypt. I've heard their cry of injustice because of their slave masters. I know about their pain. I've come down to rescue them from the Egyptians in order to take them out of that land and bring them to a good and broad land, a land that's full of milk and honey, a place where the Canaanites, the Hittites, the Amorites, the Perizzites, the Hivites, and the Jebusites all live. Now the Israelites' cries of injustice have reached me. I've seen just how much the Egyptians have oppressed them. So get going. I'm sending you to Pharaoh to bring my people, the Israelites, out of Egypt."

CONNECT HEAD AND HEART

> How do you think you would have felt seeing something like a burning bush, experiencing the presence of something supernatural?

> Are there places you've been that felt sacred or holy to you? What was it about the place that felt so special?

> Why do you think Moses made excuses as to why he couldn't be the one to do what God was calling him to do?

> Have you ever felt like you were supposed to do something but also felt like you couldn't do it? What kind of excuses did you give? What happened?

But Moses said to God, "Who am I to go to Pharaoh and to bring the Israelites out of Egypt?"

God said, "I'll be with you. And this will show you that I'm the one who sent you. After you bring the people out of Egypt, you will come back here and worship God on this mountain."

But Moses said to God, "If I now come to the Israelites and say to them, 'The God of your ancestors has sent me to you,' they are going to ask me, 'What's this God's name?' What am I supposed to say to them?"

God said to Moses, "I Am Who I Am. So say to the Israelites, 'I Am has sent me to you.'" God continued, "Say to the Israelites, 'The LORD, the God of your ancestors, Abraham's God, Isaac's God, and Jacob's God, has sent me to you.' This is my name forever; this is how all generations will remember me.

REFLECT

The beginning chapters of the book of Exodus tell the story of the Israelite people and their situation in slavery. Into that circumstance, Moses is born. Moses belonged to the people of Israel, but he was raised in the palace of the Pharaoh, the person who was currently enslaving the Israelite people and making them work to provide for the good of Egypt.

In some ways, Moses was lost. He was off course. He was struggling to figure out his place in the world. He is in a desert place, which in the Bible often becomes a place where people have an encounter with God.

At the point this story picks up, Moses has run away from Egypt because he committed a crime in defense of his people. He's now hiding out with the Midianite people. He got married and was taking care of his father-in-law's flocks.

In some ways, Moses was lost. He was off course. He was struggling to figure out his place in the world. He is in a desert place, which in the Bible often becomes a place where people have an encounter with God.

While Moses is tending to the flock he sees a bush that is burning. But it's not on fire and burning up, it's burning continuously. Now obviously this is quite a sight and Moses wants to figure out what's going on. As he gets closer he hears a voice calling to him out of the bush.

The voice tells Moses to take off his shoes because he is standing on holy ground. The voice (which we'll find out in a moment is the voice of God) wants Moses to understand that something special is happening here. Moses needs to tread lightly, to pay attention, to honor this moment as sacred. Sacred means that something is set apart, it's for special use, and in this moment it's the bush and the ground surrounding it that has been set apart for this special moment.

God reveals God's identity, telling Moses that the one who is now speaking from the bush is the God of Moses' ancestors. Moses hides his face.

Seeing God must have been pretty intense, but I also wonder if Moses is ashamed of the crime he committed back in Egypt. If he's worried he's going to get into trouble for running away and leaving his people. If he is feeling unworthy of God's attention.

God goes on to tell Moses that God has heard the cry of the people. God has seen all of the bad things that are happening to them and God is going to do something about it—and wants Moses to be the leader of the mission. God wants Moses to go to Pharaoh, the King of Egypt, and tell him to "Let my people go."

Moses, instead of being honored and excited, immediately comes up with excuses. Who am I to do this? God assures Moses he won't be alone. Moses comes up with another excuse: "If I tell the people, they're not going to believe me. So I'm going to need a name for you." God gives Moses a name, but still the list of Moses' excuses roll on.

CONNECT HEART AND HANDS

- **Do some research on young people who have made a difference in the world. What compelled them to do the work they did? How did they do it even though they were young? Share what you learnt with a friend or a trusted adult.**
- **Is there something you wish you could change in your community? What action can you take to start that change this week?**

The story continues with Moses finally agreeing to go. At every step of the way God fulfills God's promises and helps Moses to do what he's called to do. Moses ends up being the one (with the help of his brother, Aaron, and his sister, Miriam) to lead the people out of slavery and into a new life.

It can be easy to feel like we can't do things that matter. We're too young, we don't have enough experience, we don't have enough power, no one is going to listen to us.

We are all capable of making some kind of difference wherever we are, with whatever gifts we have. We just have to have the courage to start.

SINGING A SONG OF VICTORY

Exodus 15:1–21

READ

Then Moses and the Israelites sang this song to the LORD:
I will sing to the LORD, for an overflowing victory!
Horse and rider he threw into the sea!
The Lord is my strength and my power;
he has become my salvation.
This is my God, whom I will praise,
the God of my ancestors, whom I will acclaim.
The LORD is a warrior;
the LORD is his name.
Pharaoh's chariots and his army he hurled into the sea;
his elite captains were sunk in the Reed Sea.
The deep sea covered them;
they sank into the deep waters like a stone.
Your strong hand, LORD, is dominant in power;
your strong hand, LORD, shatters the enemy!
Who is like you among the gods, LORD?
Who is like you, foremost in holiness,
worthy of highest praise, doing awesome deeds?
You raised your strong hand;
earth swallowed them up.

With your great loyalty you led the people you rescued;
with your power you guided them to your sanctuary.
The peoples heard, they shook in terror;
horror grabbed hold of Philistia's inhabitants.
Then Edom's tribal chiefs were terrified;
panic grabbed hold of Moab's rulers;
all of Canaan's inhabitants melted in fear.
Terror and fear came over them;
because of your great power,
they were as still as a stone
until your people, LORD, passed by,
until the people you made your own passed by.
You brought them in and planted them on your own mountain,
the place, LORD, that you made your home,
the sanctuary, LORD, that your hand created.
The LORD will rule forever and always.
When Pharaoh's horses, chariots, and cavalry went into the sea, the LORD brought back the waters of the sea over them. But the Israelites walked through the sea on dry ground.
Then the prophet Miriam, Aaron's sister, took a tambourine in her hand. All the women followed her playing tambourines and dancing. Miriam sang the refrain back to them:
Sing to the LORD, for an overflowing victory!
Horse and rider he threw into the sea!

REFLECT

After Moses and Aaron and Miriam lead their people out of Egypt and across the Reed Sea, they finally, truly, feel like they are free. And their first impulse? Break into song!

This isn't a musical, but Moses sings a song of victory, recounting what has happened and praising God for the people's freedom.

CONNECT HEAD AND HEART

> Why do you think Moses was moved to sing a song after the people were freed?

> Thinking about Miriam packing a tambourine in her bags, what "non-essentials" would you want to have with you if you had to leave your home suddenly?

> Have there been pieces of art that moved you or comforted you when you were going through a hard time? What were they? How did they help?

And then Miriam, the sister of Moses and Aaron, pulls out a tambourine and the women join with her and they dance and sing and celebrate!

There's something really striking about this moment. We can picture the people singing and dancing, reveling in their freedom. What a change in mood from just a short while before when they were fleeing in terror and being pursued by their captors.

But there's something else that I love about this story. This group of people had to leave their homes quickly and set out on a journey into an unknown future and in an unknown territory. They had to carry everything with them, so the instructions would have been to pack light and only bring the essentials.

And Miriam considered her tambourine an essential!

Our society sometimes devalues art. We put a lot of money into sports programs in schools, but we cut theatre and music programs. We sometimes act as if art is frivolous. But when we look at movements for social justice, art and artists are often at the front.

Our society sometimes devalues art. We put a lot of money into sports programs in schools, but we cut theatre and music programs. We sometimes act as if art is frivolous. But when we look at movements for social justice, art and artists are often at the front.

From the singing of protest songs, to films that help us to see and understand people from communities who are different from us, to the use of murals and street art to send a message, artists are often essential to movements of justice. Not just as comfort, but also to push and energize the work, to set the tone, and to help us dream about the future we're trying to bring about.

When Miriam packed the tambourine in her bag she was believing, already, that there was going to be a time in the near future when they would get to celebrate.

And that's often what artists can help us do: picture the future, and help us celebrate when we get there. What a powerful thing.

CONNECT HEART AND HANDS

- Think of a time when you overcame something hard and then write a song about it!
- Watch a film about a heroic figure, or listen to a piece of music about a momentous moment in history. Some ideas: The movies *Selma, Crip Camp, Beans.* Music like *What's Going On* by Marvin Gaye, *Strange Fruit* by Billie Holiday, *Baraye* by Shervin Hajipour, *Wo Fie* by Angel Maxine featuring Wanlov the Kubolor & Sister Deborah.
- Find out more about how women have supported movements (even if they weren't the ones who got the main credit). Some examples to get you started: Harriet Tubman, Fannie Lou Hamer, Ida B. Wells-Barnett, and Wangari Maathai.

GIDEON TESTS GOD

Judges 6:11–18

READ

Then the Lord's messenger came and sat under the oak at Ophrah that belonged to Joash the Abiezrite. His son Gideon was threshing wheat in a winepress to hide it from the Midianites. The Lord's messenger appeared to him and said, "The Lord is with you, mighty warrior!"

But Gideon replied to him, "With all due respect, my Lord, if the Lord is with us, why has all this happened to us? Where are all his amazing works that our ancestors recounted to us, saying, 'Didn't the Lord bring us up from Egypt?' But now the Lord has abandoned us and allowed Midian to overpower us."

Then the Lord turned to him and said, "You have strength, so go and rescue Israel from the power of Midian. Am I not personally sending you?"

But again Gideon said to him, "With all due respect, my Lord, how can I rescue Israel? My clan is the weakest in Manasseh, and I'm the youngest in my household."

The Lord replied, "Because I'm with you, you'll defeat the Midianites as if they were just one person."

CONNECT HEAD AND HEART

> What do you think about Gideon's back and forth with the messenger?

> What do you think about Gideon asking God for a sign in order to prove what God is saying?

> Have you ever wondered about God's plan or asked God for a sign? What happened?

Then Gideon said to him, "If I've gained your approval, please show me a sign that it's really you speaking with me. Don't leave here until I return, bring out my offering, and set it in front of you."

The LORD replied, "I'll stay until you return."

REFLECT

The book of Judges is a series of stories about the Israelite people getting into trouble and God getting them out of it.

In this story the Israelite people are being ruled by the Midianite people. Gideon is trying to work, providing for his family, but he's hiding in order to protect himself.

A messenger of the Lord appears to Gideon and calls him a mighty warrior and tells him that God is with him. Gideon's first response is to bring the messenger to task. He's really blunt with his feelings, saying if God was REALLY with them then why are they in this terrible situation? Gideon is basically saying, "You know, God has done great things for our people in the past, but now?

Now we're in this terrible spot. I don't know if I believe God is with us."

The messenger's response: "You save the people."

That is probably NOT what Gideon wanted to hear. He was waiting on a miracle and the messenger said HE was the one he'd been waiting for. Gideon immediately offers excuses: My family isn't very powerful. I'm the youngest. And his response makes sense. That's often how we respond when someone asks us to do something that's outside of our comfort zone. We make excuses. We tell them why we're not the person who can do that.

But the messenger says, "If I'm with you, you can do it."

Gideon then tries another tactic: Show me a sign. Prove to me that you're with me. And the messenger agrees.

Often we worry that we're not capable of doing great things. Maybe because of our age, or because of our family, or because of the things we consider weaknesses. But over and over, the stories in the Bible tell us that God uses unexpected people to do great things.

As the story goes on, Gideon tests God multiple times and every time the test shows that God is with him. Then he becomes the one who leads not a massive army but a very small band of dedicated people, and he ends up freeing the Israelite people.

From the youngest person in a weak family came a mighty victory.

Often we worry that we're not capable of doing great things. Maybe because of our age, or because of our family, or because of the things we consider weaknesses. But over and over, the stories in the Bible tell us that God uses unexpected people to do great things.

CONNECT HEART AND HANDS

- **Make a list of things other people might consider weaknesses but that you consider your superpowers.**
- **Research some unlikely heroes. What made them unlikely? What did they do to make the world a better place? Here are some people to get you started: Ruby Bridges, Malala Yousafzai, Bayard Rustin, Pauli Murray.**

How might the things you consider weaknesses actually end up being your superpowers? Maybe your age is something that helps you to see things in new ways. Maybe your family life has taught you how to make great things out of not a lot of materials. Maybe your lack of strength has shown you how to use your words or your intellect to make change happen.

No matter who you are, you can play a part in working for the liberation of all people.

A COMFORT POEM

Psalm 23

READ

The LORD is my shepherd.
I lack nothing.
He lets me rest in grassy meadows;
he leads me to restful waters;
he keeps me alive.
He guides me in proper paths
for the sake of his good name.
Even when I walk through the darkest valley,
I fear no danger because you are with me.
Your rod and your staff—
they protect me.
You set a table for me
right in front of my enemies.
You bathe my head in oil;
my cup is so full it spills over!
Yes, goodness and faithful love
will pursue me all the days of my life,
and I will live in the LORD's house
as long as I live.

REFLECT

The Psalms are a collection of texts that were probably poems or songs. Many of them were written by David who started out as a shepherd and became the King of Israel. He wrote poems to express his feelings, to share his experiences with God, and to say things that maybe couldn't be said another way.

These poems became important in Jewish ritual and worship; many of them were put to music and sung. Jesus and his followers would have used these Psalms as prayers and sung them in worship. Words were passed down from generation to generation, and continue to be passed to us today.

CONNECT HEAD AND HEART

> **What feelings does this psalm bring up in you? What images in it do you find most comforting? Least comforting?**

> **What do you imagine Jesus would have loved about this psalm?**

> **Have you ever tried to write poetry or a song? How did it go? How did working on it feel?**

> **What is your favorite song? Why do you love it so much?**

Over the years, many, many people have turned to the Psalms for comfort and inspiration. In some communities people pray the Psalms every day. In others, they sing them. There's something about these ancient songs that still resonate for us today. They make room for a large range of emotions, including ones that are hard, like anger, grief, and pain.

We can rest in these promises. We can know there is space with God to share all of our emotions AND that we are not alone in feeling them. We can also know that generations of people have turned to these same words in their own times of fear.

This particular psalm is one of the most famous. It's the one people turn to when they are feeling afraid, sad, or facing something difficult. Even though many of us have different experiences from David (most of us aren't shepherds!) there is something in here that feels universal.

It's like when you listen to a song and feel it was written just for you. You don't know the songwriter, but somehow they've managed to tap in to something that is deeply personal. It helps you to feel seen and comforted.

This psalm assures us of God's presence. It says that even when we are facing hard things we are not alone. While some of the images might be foreign to us, we can still get a sense of what David was trying to communicate.

CONNECT HEART AND HANDS

- Rewrite this psalm using imagery that's comforting to you.
- Go to YouTube and listen to some song versions of this psalm.
- Write a poem or a song that expresses how you feel about God.
- Ask someone what their favorite song is and listen to it together. Then share your favorite song.

We have images of comfort and presence, of abundance and safety, of community and celebration. The psalm paints a picture of a God who is intimately connected and concerned about God's people, who leads and guides them with love.

We can rest in these promises. We can know there is space with God to share all of our emotions AND that we are not alone in feeling them. We can also know that generations of people have turned to these same words in their own times of fear.

A WORD FROM A PROPHET

Isaiah 61

READ

The LORD God's spirit is upon me,
because the LORD has anointed me.
He has sent me
to bring good news to the poor,
to bind up the brokenhearted,
to proclaim release for captives,
and liberation for prisoners,
to proclaim the year of the LORD's favor
and a day of vindication for our God,
to comfort all who mourn,
to provide for Zion's mourners,
to give them a crown in place of ashes,
oil of joy in place of mourning,
a mantle of praise in place of discouragement.
They will be called Oaks of Righteousness,
planted by the LORD to glorify himself.
They will rebuild the ancient ruins;
they will restore formerly deserted places;
they will renew ruined cities,
places deserted in generations past.

CONNECT HEAD AND HEART

> Look again at the first twelve lines of this passage. If those things happened, what would that look like in the world?

> Have you ever experienced consequences for doing something (or not doing something)? What happened? How did it make you feel?

> So much of this text is about how the people of Zion will be a benefit to the people around them. How would your faith be different if you looked at it as mainly about making the lives of others better? What are some things you might do differently?

> How does your faith benefit the people around you?

Foreigners will stay and shepherd your sheep,
and strangers will be your farmers and vinedressers.
You will be called The Priests of the LORD;
Ministers of Our God, they will say about you.
You will feed on the wealth of nations,
and fatten yourself on their riches.
Instead of shame, their portion will be double;
instead of disgrace, they will rejoice over their share.
They will possess a double portion in their land;
everlasting joy will be theirs.
I, the LORD, love justice;
I hate robbery and dishonesty.
I will faithfully give them their wage,
and make with them an enduring covenant.
Their offspring will be known among the nations,
and their descendants among the peoples.

All who see them will recognize
that they are a people blessed by the LORD.

REFLECT

Isaiah is a prophet. In this text he tells us that God's Spirit is on him and has anointed him to send a message to the people of Israel (in this passage, called Zion).

The message that Isaiah is given is a message of hope to a people who were discouraged. This particular text is actually connected to the chapters that come before and after it. They are meant to be taken all together, so we have to do a bit of work to understand why and how it relates to the other chapters.

Once again, the people of Israel are in exile, meaning they've been captured by another country and taken away from their homes. The prophet is coming to give them an explanation. In the chapters before this, Isaiah lays out that the people have turned away from following God, and because they'd stopped doing the things they were supposed to do, the consequences of their actions are their current state. Sometimes people will read a passage like this and say that God is punishing the people for their disobedience, but it's more helpful to think of this as consequences. It's like when adults tell you you won't be able to play sports if you don't get your grades up. If you get kicked off the team, it might feel like a punishment, but in reality it was because you didn't uphold what you were supposed to do.

So Isaiah is telling the people they've messed up. They've turned away from the things they knew they were supposed to be doing and now they are suffering the consequences. BUT! There is hope. If the people turn away from those bad behaviors, God tells them there will be good consequences. This text from Isaiah 61 is the promise.

Isaiah is telling the people they've messed up. They've turned away from the things they knew they were supposed to be doing and now they are suffering the consequences. BUT! There is hope.

This text is all about concrete good things: good news to the poor, comfort for people with broken hearts, freedom for prisoners, the year of the Lord's favor (which was a year when all debts would be forgiven and land would be returned to its original owners so no one could end up with generational poverty), comfort for people who mourn, the list goes on.

But it's not just promises about good things happening to the people of Israel, it's also that they will be a blessing to the people around them. They'll help to rebuild ruins and renew cities, there will be people from other nations who want to come and help them and be a part of their community, they will be an example and a blessing to the people around them. (In fact, Jesus uses this text hundreds of years later when he announces what he has come to do in the world!)

Sometimes we think about our faith, or doing the right things, as just between us and God—it's private or something we do to keep us in God's favor. But over and over, the Bible encourages us that our faith is about our relationships with other people. How are we being helpful to the people around us? How are we bringing healing to other people? How are we encouraging peace and right relationships?

Our faith brings us comfort, but it also helps us to bring comfort to others. As we do the right things, the things that lead to peace and justice, we will be a part of bringing healing to our communities.

CONNECT HEART AND HANDS

- **There is a lot of beautiful imagery in this passage: "They will be called Oaks of Righteousness," "They will rebuild the ancient ruins," "a crown in place of ashes," etc. Pick one or two of the images and either draw a picture or look up some photos online and explore how the pictures help you to understand this text more fully.**
- **Look into the work of the Innocence Project, an organization working to free people who are unjustly incarcerated. What are some things you might be able to do to support their work (or work like theirs)?**
- **There is a line in this text that says "they will renew ruined cities." What are some things you could do to renew the area around you this week?**

SPEAK TO THE BONES

Ezekiel 37:1–14

READ

The LORD's power overcame me, and while I was in the LORD's spirit, he led me out and set me down in the middle of a certain valley. It was full of bones. He led me through them all around, and I saw that there were a great many of them on the valley floor, and they were very dry.

He asked me, "Human one, can these bones live again?"

I said, "LORD God, only you know."

He said to me, "Prophesy over these bones, and say to them, Dry bones, hear the LORD's word! The LORD God proclaims to these bones: I am about to put breath in you, and you will live again. I will put sinews on you, place flesh on you, and cover you with skin. When I put breath in you, and you come to life, you will know that I am the LORD."

I prophesied just as I was commanded. There was a great noise as I was prophesying, then a great quaking, and the bones came together, bone by bone. When I looked, suddenly there were sinews on them. The flesh appeared, and then they were covered over with skin. But there was still no breath in them.

He said to me, "Prophesy to the breath; prophesy, human one! Say to the breath, The LORD God proclaims: Come from the four winds, breath! Breathe into these dead bodies and let them live."

I prophesied just as he commanded me. When the breath entered them, they came to life and stood on their feet, an extraordinarily large company.

CONNECT HEAD AND HEART

> What do you think it would have been like to have this vision like Ezekiel did?

> How do you think the people would have felt when they heard Ezekiel's message?

> What do you think it would have been like to be a prophet? If you had to give a word of hope to a person or a community who was feeling hopeless, what would you say?

> What would be the most hopeful thing someone could say to you right now? What would make hearing that so special?

He said to me, "Human one, these bones are the entire house of Israel. They say, 'Our bones are dried up, and our hope has perished. We are completely finished.' So now, prophesy and say to them, The LORD God proclaims: I'm opening your graves! I will raise you up from your graves, my people, and I will bring you to Israel's fertile land. You will know that I am the LORD, when I open your graves and raise you up from your graves, my people.I will put my breath in you, and you will live. I will plant you on your fertile land, and you will know that I am the LORD. I've spoken, and I will do it. This is what the LORD says."

REFLECT

Ezekiel is another one of a series of prophets, called by God to bring some kind of message to the community of Israel. Sometimes prophets were called to warn the people to change their behavior because they were heading down a dangerous road; sometimes prophets were called to give the people a message about what God was going to do next; and sometimes, like in this text, prophets were called to bring a message of hope.

Our story today is about Ezekiel having a fantastic vision, but to understand why this vision matters we have to know a bit more about what's going in.

Sometimes, in order to feel and be revived, we need someone to speak a good and holy word to us. And sometimes we are called on to speak that word of encouragement and hope to others.

The people of Israel, at this time, were in exile—their nation had been taken over by another nation and they were taken away from their homeland and forced to live somewhere else. Sometimes they were put to work, sometimes they were simply dropped somewhere else. It was very disruptive. It took people away from their communities, from their land, and from their religious practices and traditions. This had happened several times over the course of their history, but this time they were in exile for a long time.

The longer they were away from their homeland, the more they began to wonder if they would ever get back there. But life kept on going: people got married, babies were born, people got older and died.

As exile went on, those who had lost family members started to lose hope. If they ever got out of exile, what would happen to their loved ones who had died and were buried in this strange land? Would they have to leave them behind? Would they be separated forever?

It's into THIS moment that Ezekiel is given a vision of a vast field of really dry bones. I can imagine he did NOT think this was a very comforting or hopeful vision at first.

God asks Ezekiel if the bones can live again. I wonder what Ezekiel thought of that question. Was he frustrated? Annoyed? Hopeful? Hopeless? His response—"Lord God, only you know"—doesn't tell us much.

So God tells him to speak to the bones. There is a great rattling and the bones reconnect, and there are muscles and sinews and skin and all of the things that make bodies, bodies . . . except for the breath.

God tells Ezekiel to call on the four winds, and he does, and the breath of life comes back into the bodies!

God says, "These bones are the entire house of Israel." Meaning, no one will be left behind. Everyone is accounted for. No one has been forgotten. What a word to receive!

God not only heard their fears and concerns but answered them with resounding hope.

There are two beautiful messages in this story: God sees us and we are not alone or forgotten. Whatever is going on in our lives, whatever is happening, we won't be left behind.

But also, sometimes, in order to feel and be revived, we need someone to speak a good and holy word to us. And sometimes we are called on to speak that word of encouragement and hope to others.

So be on the lookout for someone who is feeling lost and alone who you can speak a word of hope to. And know that God is with you wherever you go.

CONNECT HEART AND HANDS

- **Leave a note of encouragement somewhere in your community. (Some ideas: something with chalk on the sidewalk, a sign in your yard, a note on someone's locker.)**
- **Do something special to remember and honor someone you love who has died (it can even be someone you don't know personally). (Some ideas: visit their grave and leave a memento, tell a story about them to someone you love, ask someone who knew them to tell you a story you've never heard before, or to retell you one of your favorite stories, look at some photos of them.)**

WHAT GOD REQUIRES

Micah 6:1–8

READ

Hear what the LORD is saying:
Arise, lay out the lawsuit before the mountains;
let the hills hear your voice!
Hear, mountains, the lawsuit of the LORD!
Hear, eternal foundations of the earth!
The LORD has a lawsuit against his people;
with Israel he will argue.
"My people, what did I ever do to you?
How have I wearied you? Answer me!
I brought you up out of the land of Egypt;
I redeemed you from the house of slavery.
I sent Moses, Aaron, and Miriam before you.
My people, remember what Moab's King Balak had planned,
and how Balaam, Beor's son, answered him!
Remember everything from Shittim to Gilgal,
that you might learn to recognize the righteous acts of the Lord!"
With what should I approach the LORD
and bow down before God on high?

Should I come before him with entirely burned offerings,
with year-old calves?
Will the LORD be pleased with thousands of rams,
with many torrents of oil?
Should I give my oldest child for my crime;
the fruit of my body for the sin of my spirit?
He has told you, human one, what is good and
what the LORD requires from you:
to do justice, embrace faithful love, and walk humbly with your God.

CONNECT HEAD AND HEART

> Have you ever experienced something that felt like a punishment but was really the consequence of your own action? What happened? When did you realize that you played a part in the situation?

> If God were making a case to tell you how God has shown up in your life, what situations would be used as evidence?

> Have you ever tried something extreme to please God? Why did you feel like you needed to do that?

REFLECT

Our passage today comes from the book of Micah. Micah is one of the prophets in the Hebrew Scriptures. Like we talked about in the story of Gideon from the book of Judges, this was a time when the people of Israel would stop following God's commands and as a result of their behavior end up in situations that were painful.

These situations weren't the result of punishment—God didn't send the people into harsh situations to punish them—these were more consequences of their own actions, like we talked about in our reading from Isaiah.

In this passage God is kind of frustrated with the people of Israel. We can imagine that they were maybe blaming God as they found themselves in a situation they didn't like, accusing God of abandoning them. The prophet tells us that God is laying out a case against the people and then proceeds to remind them of all of the times God has been faithful to them and showed up for them: when God gave them leaders to free them from slavery in Egypt, and when God rescued them from other leaders who wanted to do them harm.

The prophet is making a point. You don't have to do all of these extravagant things; God has already told you what you're supposed to do: do justice, embrace faithful love, and walk humbly with God.

Then the prophet responds by asking what kind of offerings the people could bring to please God. They ask about different offerings and sacrifices. They even talk about offering their children! It's kind of extreme. But the prophet is making a point. You don't have to do all of these extravagant things; God has already told you what you're supposed to do: do justice, embrace faithful love, and walk humbly with God.

This story is a reminder to us of a couple of things. First, God's faithfulness to us: rescuing us, keeping us safe, leading us toward ways of community where we'll have what we need.

CONNECT HEART AND HANDS

- **Find one thing you can do this week to do justice in your neighborhood.**
- **Find one thing you can do this week to embrace faithful love.**
- **Find one way to walk humbly with God this week.**

And it's also a reminder of our responsibilities as followers of God: to play our part in bringing about justice where we are, to embracing love (of God, of ourselves, and of those around us), and to walk with God humbly (paying attention to others and doing what God asks).

Sometimes we feel like we have to do a lot to please God. We go all out. We try to really impress with our devotion. But we don't have to do the extreme things; it's not about getting it perfect or making huge gestures. What God really wants is a lot more simple. Looking out for our neighbors, loving our community, being quietly faithful. It's in the pursuit of justice.

INTRODUCTION TO THE CHRISTIAN SCRIPTURES

The Christian Scriptures (often called the New Testament) are made up of twenty-seven books. There are several different types of books in this set of twenty-seven: the Gospels, the book of Acts (sometimes combined with the Gospels), a whole bunch of letters, and the book of Revelation. The Gospels, Acts, and Revelation are more narrative in style, meaning they tell a story or a collection of stories. The letters are just that, letters written by a person to another person or community. As we get to each of those sections we'll talk more about how to read the different types of books.

The Christian Scriptures give us an idea of how Christianity started, how it grew, and what the most important things in our faith are. We are invited to "come and see" (and to join!) the continued work of this movement!

Most of the books in the Christian Scriptures are focused on the story of Jesus and the beginning of the Christian Church. Jesus was Jewish. He was raised Jewish and brought up in the Jewish tradition. He was dedicated and named in the temple, visited the teachers as a young boy, celebrated festivals, and participated in the worshipping life of his community.

In many ways, Jesus came in the tradition of the Jewish prophets: seeking to bring people back to the heart of Judaism and telling them how God wanted them to behave—and it wasn't until after his death and resurrection that people really realized just how special his message was.

As the message of Jesus spreads, particularly after his death and resurrection, a lot of people wanted to follow Jesus and some of those people were not from the Jewish tradition. The Christian Scriptures record the story of how a Jewish movement becomes a Christian movement as people from different backgrounds argue about the best ways to follow Jesus.

As we read we need to pay attention to the fact that these stories are about a new community trying to figure out their identity. At the time these stories were written, most of this was in-fighting between groups who considered themselves to be part of the same tradition (and both groups were under the rule of Rome which wasn't very kind to them).

The Christian Scriptures give us an idea of how Christianity started, how it grew, and what the most important things in our faith are. We are invited to "come and see" (and to join!) the continued work of this movement!

INTRODUCTION TO THE GOSPELS

The first four books of the Christian Scriptures (also called the New Testament) are called the Gospels. Each Gospel is named after a person: Matthew, Mark, Luke, and John. Each of these Gospels is a standalone account of the life and ministry of Jesus. The book of Acts is sometimes paired with the Gospel of Luke because it picks up where that story leaves off. These five books tell stories about Jesus and the formation of the Christian Church.

Some traditions say that these Gospels were named after the person who wrote them, but most scholars don't think that's the case because of issues with dating the texts (among other things). Instead, these stories were written by unknown authors and named after people who were important to the early Jesus followers.

Scholars call the first three Gospels (Matthew, Mark, and Luke) the synoptic Gospels because they share a lot of the same stories and were probably written with some shared sources. Even with those shared sources, though, the writers each chose which stories to include and which details to change or shift.

The Gospel of John uses a lot of new material and leaves out many of the stories in the synoptic Gospels.

John was written much later than the first three Gospels and worked to spiritualize or theologize many of the stories. John's Gospel was written at a time when many of the people who had known and worked with Jesus were no longer alive. The ideas about who Jesus was and what his life meant were beginning to shift the further people got from his time on earth.

Each of the Gospel stories of Jesus was written to a particular people in a particular place in a particular time. Because of that, each of the writers chose different things to emphasize. They were telling stories about Jesus, but they were also using those stories to reflect on what was happening in their own communities as they were writing.

These four books (and the book of Acts) help us to better understand who Jesus was and what he meant to the people who followed him. They give us a picture of how the Christian Church started and how they formed communities. They also help us to understand how different communities understood the life and ministry of Jesus and how those understandings impacted how they lived out their faith. We, too, are invited to consider how we might live out OUR faith today.

A DUDE WITH WEIRD CLOTHES

Matthew 3:1–12

READ

In those days John the Baptist appeared in the desert of Judea announcing, "Change your hearts and lives! Here comes the kingdom of heaven!" He was the one of whom Isaiah the prophet spoke when he said:

The voice of one shouting in the wilderness,
"Prepare the way for the Lord;
make his paths straight."

John wore clothes made of camel's hair, with a leather belt around his waist. He ate locusts and wild honey.

People from Jerusalem, throughout Judea, and all around the Jordan River came to him. As they confessed their sins, he baptized them in the Jordan River. Many Pharisees and Sadducees came to be baptized by John. He said to them, "You children of snakes! Who warned you to escape from the angry judgment that is coming soon? Produce fruit that shows you have changed your hearts and lives. And don't even think about saying to yourselves, Abraham is our father. I tell you that God is able to raise up Abraham's children from these stones. The ax is already at the root of the trees. Therefore, every tree that doesn't produce good fruit will be chopped down and tossed into the fire. I baptize with water those of you who have changed your hearts and lives. The one who is coming after me is stronger than I am. I'm not worthy to carry his sandals. He will baptize you with the Holy Spirit and with fire."

REFLECT

One of the first things people often talk about with this passage is the fact that John wore clothing made of camel's hair and ate locusts and wild honey! To be sure, it's a rather remarkable kind of thing to eat! But it wasn't just what he ate or his clothing that made people pay attention to John. He was someone who was part of a group of people who dedicated their lives to God and who showed that dedication in the way they dressed, the food they ate, and by living in their own communities away from the rest of society.

In the Gospel of Matthew, we are told the story of Jesus' birth and then we jump ahead in chapter three to John. John (who is actually Jesus' cousin) enters into the story with a big announcement. He calls on people to change their hearts and lives, to prepare for something exciting that is about to happen.

The writer of Matthew tells us that John is part of the prophetic tradition. Prophets usually show up when things are messed up. They look around and they see that if we don't change how we're behaving we're going to be in trouble. Like the activists from Parkland High School who asked the government to do something about school shootings, or Greta Thunberg who told us to pay attention to the climate crisis.

CONNECT HEAD AND HEART

> Do you have things that are particular to your religious practice, such as clothing, things you use for prayer, etc.? What do they mean to you?

> Can you think of anyone else you might consider a prophet? (Maybe someone like Martin Luther King Jr., Sylvia Rivera, Noga Levy Rapoport, or Jazz Jennings.)

> What is the message the prophets on your list are trying to get us to hear?

> How do people respond to those prophets and their message?

> Why do you think it's hard to listen to people who are prophets?

Prophets show up, they point out the problem, and they invite people to change so they can be part of the solution. Sometimes these people can seem angry. They might yell or tell people they are doing things wrong. This anger comes, often, from deep grief about the way things are. These prophets are sad about the damage that has already been done, they are afraid for the future if we don't change, and they want people to know that change is possible. Sometimes, because of their passion or their anger, people are afraid of them or don't like them. Sometimes, like John, they wear clothing or do things that make a statement and get attention. (Like Greta Thunberg's **School Strike for Climate** protest. When she was in high school she sat outside, every day, to bring attention to the climate crisis. She often sat alone, in all kinds of weather, because she wanted people to pay attention.)

John reminds us that there are always prophets in our midst. There are always people who can see the problems in the world and want to invite us to consider how we can be part of the solution.

John was doing the same. He was trying to bring people's attention to what wasn't working. They were living in a time when the people in charge were oppressing the Jewish community (of which both John and Jesus were a part). They were in a place where there was a lot of poverty, where the divide between the rich and the poor just got bigger and bigger. There was violence and some people didn't have enough to eat. John believed there could be another way and he wanted the people to change their hearts and their lives so they could take care of one another better. He knew that Jesus was going to show the community how to do that, and he wanted people to be ready to listen to Jesus when he started his ministry.

John reminds us that there are always prophets in our midst. There are always people who can see the problems in the world and want to invite us to consider how we can be part of the solution.

CONNECT HEART AND HANDS

- Pick one of the prophets on your list and listen to some of the speeches they've given.
- If there is a call to action in one of the speeches, can you do it?
- Find a cause you care about and do some digging to see what you can do to be helpful.
- Tell someone else something you've learnt about the cause you care about.

Who are the prophets in your life? Who is speaking loudly, right now, about things that are messed up? What are they asking us to do to be a part of making things better?

JESUS' BAPTISM

Matthew 3:13–17

READ

At that time Jesus came from Galilee to the Jordan River so that John would baptize him. John tried to stop him and said, "I need to be baptized by you, yet you come to me?" Jesus answered, "Allow me to be baptized now. This is necessary to fulfill all righteousness." So John agreed to baptize Jesus. When Jesus was baptized, he immediately came up out of the water. Heaven was opened to him, and he saw the Spirit of God coming down like a dove and resting on him. A voice from heaven said, "This is my Son whom I dearly love; I find happiness in him."

REFLECT

John started his ministry as part of the legacy of prophets, people who remind us that we can and should do better. He was also reminding people that someone greater, a leader, was coming, and in this section of the story, that leader arrives.

In the Gospel of Matthew, Jesus is born, a couple of years later the magi visit him and his family, and then we don't hear about him again until this moment. Jesus, now an adult, re-enters the story.

CONNECT HEAD AND HEART

> What are some symbols in your life?

> What do you think it would have been like for John to baptize his cousin?

> What do you think it would have meant to Jesus to hear that voice from heaven?

> If you go to a church, how does your church do baptisms?

> Have you been baptized? Why or why not?

> What does the idea of baptism mean to you?

Jesus knows of John, because they were cousins, but probably also because of the prophetic ministry John was engaged in. Jesus goes to John to be baptized as a symbol that his public ministry is about to start.

Symbols are really important. They help people to be united. Think about how sports fans wear jerseys from their favorite teams and players to signal to others who they cheer for. They help us to recognize one another. Think about people wearing a rainbow bracelet or putting some kind of bumper sticker on their car with a cause they care about. They help us to mark special occasions. Think about the symbol of a birthday card or a graduation gown.

In Jewish tradition (of which both John and Jesus were a part) there is a custom of *tevilah*. This is an immersion in a body of water (it generally happens in something called a *mikvah* which allows someone to go fully under the water). Undergoing this practice was about purification. It restored you to purity under the Jewish law.

Later on, Christians took the same underlying idea—full immersion in water—and identified it as something you do when you decide to follow Jesus. The idea of baptism was to echo the idea of the death, burial, and resurrection of Jesus and to symbolize a person's new life in Christ.

Now, many different churches do baptism in a lot of different ways, from sprinkling water on a baby's head to full immersion for adults. All of these symbols are rooted, though, in this story of Jesus' baptism by John.

This moment for Jesus must have been a special one. Not only was he declaring he was finally ready to start his public ministry, he also has the experience of hearing a voice from heaven claiming him as a dearly beloved son.

This moment for Jesus must have been a special one. Not only was he declaring he was finally ready to start his public ministry, he also has the experience of hearing a voice from heaven claiming him as a dearly beloved son.

CONNECT HEART AND HANDS

- If you were baptized as a baby, ask you parents or guardians to tell you the story of your baptism. Who was there? Who spoke?
- Do a remembrance of baptism. Find some water (preferably outside, but any water will do) and make the sign of the cross on your forehead. Remember how loved by God you are.
- Make a sign that says "I am dearly loved by God" and hang it somewhere you'll see it often as a reminder of your goodness.

Later in his ministry, when he got discouraged or felt afraid or started to doubt, I wonder if he looked back on this moment and remembered the experience?

That is the power of symbols. They can remind us of things. They can remind us we're not alone. They can remind us we are prepared and knowledgeable. They can remind us what we've committed to.

JESUS WAS TEMPTED TOO

Matthew 4:1–11

READ

Then the Spirit led Jesus up into the wilderness so that the devil might tempt him. After Jesus had fasted for forty days and forty nights, he was starving. The tempter came to him and said, "Since you are God's Son, command these stones to become bread."

Jesus replied, "It's written, *People won't live only by bread, but by every word spoken by God.*"

After that the devil brought him into the holy city and stood him at the highest point of the temple. He said to him, "Since you are God's Son, throw yourself down; for it is written, *I will command my angels concerning you, and they will take you up in their hands so that you won't hit your foot on a stone.*"

Jesus replied, "Again it's written, *Don't test the Lord your God.*"

Then the devil brought him to a very high mountain and showed him all the kingdoms of the world and their glory. He said, "I'll give you all these if you bow down and worship me."

Jesus responded, "Go away, Satan, because it's written, *You will worship the Lord your God and serve only him.*" The devil left him, and angels came and took care of him.

REFLECT

Before Jesus starts his public ministry he is led by the Spirit into the wilderness. People hearing this story would have known that in the Jewish tradition the wilderness is often a place people hear God. There's something about getting away from your day-to-day life, finding some time in silence, and being alone that allows you to hear more clearly. (This is why some people love to go camping or hiking, or to spend time on silent retreats.)

CONNECT HEAD AND HEART

> **How do you think Jesus felt being all alone in the wilderness?**

> **Have you ever been alone for a long time? How did it make you feel?**

> **Have you ever been tempted to make a decision you knew wasn't the right one? What was the decision? What did you do?**

Jesus spends forty days in the wilderness. Forty is an important number in the Bible. Forty days is the amount of time it was said to rain in the time of Noah. Forty years is how long the Israelite people wandered in the wilderness. The writer of Matthew is connecting Jesus back to these important stories in the Jewish tradition, helping people to understand that Jesus matters. That he was from this tradition of prophets who will lead the people toward freedom. In this time in the wilderness Jesus fasts, meaning he doesn't eat anything. Fasting is sometimes something people do in order to help them pay more attention, to clear away the noise, and to really focus. At the end of the forty days the writer tells us Jesus was starving—and we can imagine he would be! We can also imagine that, being as hungry as he was, he was also more vulnerable. He might have been a little "hangry" too!

It's then that "the tempter" came to him. Sometimes, because of literature or artwork, we have a picture of "the devil" as a demon or person, perhaps someone all in red with a pointy tail and horns. But in the Christian Scriptures the Greek is less clear. It's about a force, a being, a temptation. It could even be something from inside the person. It's not what we sometimes picture.

I think of Jesus, in his weakened and hungry state, as he's considering starting his public ministry, a ministry which would bring him into conflict with a lot of people. He's scared. He's lonely. He's worried about getting it right. And he is met with a series of temptations.

These temptations still resonate today. As we decide what it means to follow Jesus, how we live out our faith in the world, will we use our gifts to benefit the people around us, will we do the right thing even when it's hard, and will we follow the rule of God and not the might of politicians and nations?

We have to understand a little bit about the context to really get these temptations. The first, on the surface, seems easy enough, even a little harmless. He's tempted to turn stones into bread. If he has power, shouldn't he use it to benefit himself? And therein lies the question: will Jesus use his power, his ministry, to serve his own needs or to serve the needs of others? Will he do what's right for him, or will he do what's right for the community?

The second temptation is about safety. Will he throw himself off the mountain, knowing he'll be protected? To stand up for justice, then as now, can sometimes be scary. It can sometimes put us in danger. The tempter is asking Jesus, will you do the right thing only if you are sure you won't get hurt? Will you do the right thing even if it costs you something?

CONNECT HEART AND HANDS

- **Ask an adult in your life to tell you about a time they were tempted to choose what was easy over what was right.**
- **Make a list of your values (these could be things like kindness, equality, friendship, etc.). Put it in a place you'll see it often. Next time you need to make a decision, compare your choices and see which ones line up with your values.**
- **Find a leader (maybe a pastor, a politician, a teacher) and ask them how they make hard decisions, especially when they know the decision will upset some people.**

Then finally, Jesus is offered all of the kingdoms of the world. The temptation is to grab political power. To rule like other kings rule. Jesus, instead, reveals that he's tuned in to the rule of God, a rule that is different than the rule of kings and political leaders.

After this last temptation the tempter leaves and Jesus is ready to start his ministry. He's been tested and he's decided what kind of leader he's going to be. He's going to look out for the good of the community and not use his power to benefit himself, he's going to do the right thing even when it might cost him, and he's going to follow God and not seek political might.

These temptations still resonate today. As we decide what it means to follow Jesus, how we live out our faith in the world, will we use our gifts to benefit the people around us, will we do the right thing even when it's hard, and will we follow the rule of God and not the might of politicians and nations?

We have Jesus' example to follow, and we can take courage knowing he, too, was tempted and still fulfilled his mission.

JESUS TEACHES US TO PRAY

Matthew 6:5–14

READ

"When you pray, don't be like hypocrites. They love to pray standing in the synagogues and on the street corners so that people will see them. I assure you, that's the only reward they'll get. But when you pray, go to your room, shut the door, and pray to your Father who is present in that secret place. Your Father who sees what you do in secret will reward you.

"When you pray, don't pour out a flood of empty words, as the Gentiles do. They think that by saying many words they'll be heard. Don't be like them, because your Father knows what you need before you ask. Pray like this:

Our Father who is in heaven,
uphold the holiness of your name.
Bring in your kingdom
so that your will is done on earth as it's done in heaven.
Give us the bread we need for today.
Forgive us for the ways we have wronged you,
just as we also forgive those who have wronged us.
And don't lead us into temptation,

but rescue us from the evil one.
"If you forgive others their sins, your heavenly Father
will also forgive you."

CONNECT HEAD AND HEART

> How do you pray? Alone? With family? At church? All of the above?

> How do you feel when you pray?

> What do you think about praying for things as a community instead of just for yourself?

REFLECT

As Jesus was teaching his friends, he wanted to help them connect to God. So he taught them how to pray. In these verses it might seem like Jesus is saying there's only one way to pray, but something deeper is going on here. Jesus isn't saying that you can do prayer "wrong," but he was seeing a lot of people who were trying to use prayer not to connect with God but to get attention from other people. They would be loud and showy. They would use their prayer time to talk about all of the good things they'd done in order to get other people to think how holy they are. Jesus wanted his friends to pray differently. His teaching to them has become what is widely known today as 'The Lord's Prayer'.

He teaches them a prayer they can use. There's something really striking about the prayer: every piece of it says "us" or "we." This is a prayer that reminds us we are in a community. Prayer isn't just about making sure we, personally, have what we need but that our whole community is fed, our whole community has our debts forgiven, our whole community forgives each other. It's a prayer that reminds us we're all in this together. If one person is hurting then we're all hurting.

He teaches them a prayer they can use. There's something really striking about the prayer: every piece of it says "us" or "we." This is a prayer that reminds us we are in a community.

Jesus, too, wants us to understand that God is deeply concerned with our needs. Jesus tells us to address God as Father, which isn't about God's gender, but is instead about addressing God as a parent. Someone who is close to us, someone we can trust, someone who has our best interests at heart. Not everyone has a good relationship with their fathers (or their parents in general) so if Father feels like a hard word for you, you can substitute another name. The point is to pick a word that says safety, trust, and love.

There are lots of different ways to pray. Some people pray by walking or by using beads. Some people pray using prayer books from their church. Some people pray quietly, some pray out loud.

This prayer from Jesus reminds us that no matter how we talk to God, we should be thinking about our whole community when we do. We should trust that God cares about our requests and wants us to feel connected, loved, and cared for. When we pray in this way, it also helps us to pay attention to the needs of our community and how we might help to meet them.

Prayer isn't just a private practice; it connects us to the Divine and to each other. It allows us to feel seen and heard and to put ourselves to work seeing and hearing others.

So let us pray for ourselves and for our communities.

CONNECT HEART AND HANDS

- **Experiment with different types of prayer: meditation, walking a labyrinth, using a prayer book, using prayer beads, etc.**
- **Ask your pastor, priest, or another religious leader about the prayers of your tradition.**
- **Pray with your feet by giving back to your community in some way.**
- **Look online to see how other people have interpreted the Lord's Prayer. What do you notice about all of the different versions?**

JESUS TEACHES US

Matthew 7:1–20

READ

"Don't judge, so that you won't be judged. You'll receive the same judgment you give. Whatever you deal out will be dealt out to you. Why do you see the splinter that's in your brother's or sister's eye, but don't notice the log in your own eye? How can you say to your brother or sister, 'Let me take the splinter out of your eye,' when there's a log in your eye? You deceive yourself! First take the log out of your eye, and then you'll see clearly to take the splinter out of your brother's or sister's eye. Don't give holy things to dogs, and don't throw your pearls in front of pigs. They will stomp on the pearls, then turn around and attack you.

"Ask, and you will receive. Search, and you will find. Knock, and the door will be opened to you. For everyone who asks, receives. Whoever seeks, finds. And to everyone who knocks, the door is opened. Who among you will give your children a stone when they ask for bread? Or give them a snake when they ask for fish? If you who are evil know how to give good gifts to your children, how much more will your heavenly Father give good things to those who ask him. Therefore, you should treat people in the same way that you want people to treat you; this is the Law and the Prophets.

"Go in through the narrow gate. The gate that leads to destruction is broad and the road wide, so many people enter through it. But the gate that leads to life is narrow and the road difficult, so few people find it.

CONNECT HEAD AND HEART

> What do you think it would have been like to listen to Jesus' teaching in person?

> Which one of the teachings in this section is the hardest for you to understand? Why?

> What do you think of the idea that our relationship with God and our relationships with other people are connected? How do you think they are connected?

> Have you experienced someone teaching something that led to bad fruit? What was the teaching? What was the fruit?

"Watch out for false prophets. They come to you dressed like sheep, but inside they are vicious wolves. You will know them by their fruit. Do people get bunches of grapes from thorny weeds, or do they get figs from thistles? In the same way, every good tree produces good fruit, and every rotten tree produces bad fruit. A good tree can't produce bad fruit. And a rotten tree can't produce good fruit. Every tree that doesn't produce good fruit is chopped down and thrown into the fire. Therefore, you will know them by their fruit.

REFLECT

Our Scripture passage for today is actually part of a much longer section (several chapters!) and is one of the longest recorded speeches of Jesus in the Gospels. In this speech, sometimes called the Sermon on the Mount, Jesus talks about what it looks like to be a follower of his way.

This portion of the speech or sermon has two main messages: how to be in right relationship with other people and how to make decisions about people who don't understand your faith and behavior.

These two themes almost alternate throughout our section. First, Jesus tells us to pay attention to how we're judging other people. It's easy to look at what someone else is doing and say it's wrong while completely ignoring that we, also, might be doing something wrong or harmful. Jesus urges us to pay attention to our own behavior instead of judging other people.

This portion of the speech or sermon has two main messages: how to be in right relationship with other people and how to make decisions about people who don't understand your faith and behavior.

In almost the next breath Jesus tells those listening to not throw good things to dogs or pearls to pigs. He's trying to help people listening to understand not everyone is going to be able to hear you. Not everyone will be able to see your goodness and uniqueness. Not everyone will want to listen to you talk about what you believe. Instead of trying to argue with them or forcing them to understand, just let it go. Let them go their own way while you do the things you know are right. This isn't about not listening to correction or other people's ideas, it is saying we don't have to argue about what we know to be true with people who are committed to misunderstanding us.

Jesus then tells his listeners to ask God for what they need and compares God to a good parent who wants the best for their kids. Instead of needing to earn God's favor or being afraid of God's punishment, we can think of God as the best, most generous parent, who wants us to have good things. Jesus then encourages us to treat others well. It's as if knowing God is good and compassionate and kind should encourage us to be the same, to treat others with respect and dignity and kindness. These two themes are often found together throughout the Bible: love God and love others.

Jesus then encourages people to do the hard, but right, thing. To enter through the narrow gate and to watch out for false prophets. There were, in Jesus' time, just like there is in our time, people who entice us to take the easy way out. To do what is fastest or leads to the most gain for ourselves. Jesus is saying sometimes the hard way is better. To work for the good of the climate instead of trying to get as much money as you can as quickly as you can. To work for justice even when it might cost you. To slow down and get better at something instead of turning in something that's "good enough."

There will be people who say things that sound good, or who push you to think or believe a certain way, but they aren't acting in your best interest. There might be people who say that if you don't believe a certain way or act a certain way God will punish you. Jesus encourages us to look at the fruit of those teachings. If a teaching bears bad fruit, if it leads people to being depressed or angry or mean to other people, if it leads people to hating themselves, if it leads people to persecuting others, then that is bad fruit. On the other hand, if the teachings lead toward love, toward justice, toward right relationships with other people, toward dignity, then it's good fruit.

All of these teachings from Jesus work together into a kind of code of ethics. A way to think about our decisions and our actions that lead us to a better understanding of God and a better relationship with the people around us. Our love for the people in our lives flows from our relationship with a loving God who wants the flourishing of all people.

CONNECT HEART AND HANDS

- **Spend one day consciously practicing being less judgmental. Try to cultivate understanding for people who act, think, or behave differently than you.**
- **Examine some of the beliefs in your life. Are they leading to the good fruit of action and justice? If not, how might you start to work to change your beliefs and actions?**
- **Jesus uses a lot of examples from his day to day in order to share his message. Rewrite some of his examples using stuff from YOUR day to day.**

GOD AS PARENT

Matthew 11:25–30

READ

At that time Jesus said, "I praise you, Father, Lord of heaven and earth, because you've hidden these things from the wise and intelligent and have shown them to babies. Indeed, Father, this brings you happiness.

"My Father has handed all things over to me. No one knows the Son except the Father. And nobody knows the Father except the Son and anyone to whom the Son wants to reveal him.

"Come to me, all you who are struggling hard and carrying heavy loads, and I will give you rest. Put on my yoke, and learn from me. I'm gentle and humble. And you will find rest for yourselves. My yoke is easy to bear, and my burden is light."

REFLECT

Our reading for today is the end of a longer section where Jesus is preaching and teaching. There are people who are questioning his ministry and he's trying to help them understand who he is and what he's here to do.

CONNECT HEAD AND HEART

> What do you think it would have been like for Jesus' followers to hear him refer to God as "Father?"

> How do you think Jesus' followers would have heard this message about the "yoke of God" being light?

> What image of God would make you feel closer to the Divine?

> What changes when you think of God as a kind, gentle figure who is on your side?

As we remember from our introduction to the Gospels, these stories are written about a particular time and place, but they are also written TO a particular community in a different time and place. So sometimes their concerns and anxieties are different than ours, and the way the writer is telling the story might make sense to them but be harder to understand for us.

What is clear here is that the community hearing this was feeling isolated and alienated from the communities around them. Maybe they were being persecuted or having their faith questioned. There might have been people telling them they were foolish for following Jesus. So Jesus slides in a bit of comfort to the end of this passage.

Those hearing this story become the ones to whom the mystery and promises were revealed to. It was a way of assuring the community that they were doing the right thing.

This section also shows us how personal Jesus' relationship with God is. He uses language here that is intimate; family language. He calls God his Father, but the word used here is more like "Daddy." It shows closeness. This doesn't mean that God is a man, but that Jesus was choosing a visual, something he understood, that made him feel close to God. His intimacy gives us permission to find an image that will make us feel close to God too.

Those hearing this story become the ones to whom the mystery and promises were revealed to. It was a way of assuring the community that they were doing the right thing.

Jesus also promises the people following him that God is a place of rest and comfort and that God's "yoke" is light. A yoke is something used by farmers to put two oxen together so they can pull a plow to till a field. By yoking

CONNECT HEART AND HANDS

- Using the image of God you journaled about, write/pray a prayer addressing God with this name. Then journal about how it felt.
- Explore or talk to people about other names for God (whether that's other religions, how poets/artists talk about God, or how people in your community refer to God). How do these names help us to see God differently?

them together it makes it easier for them to pull. Jesus is saying when we put our energies with the energies of the Divine it will be easier to do good work in the world.

In a time when people were living in poverty, being oppressed by the political powers around them, this promise of a light yoke was something really special.

To think of God not as a bully, not as someone who will add to their oppression, not as someone who will make it harder for them, but as a gentle parental figure who will make things easier and take care of you was a really different understanding of power and a different understanding of what it would mean to have a relationship with God.

LEARNING FROM UNEXPECTED PEOPLE

Matthew 19:11–15

READ

[Jesus] replied, "Not everybody can accept this teaching, but only those who have received the ability to accept it. For there are eunuchs who have been eunuchs from birth. And there are eunuchs who have been made eunuchs by other people. And there are eunuchs who have made themselves eunuchs because of the kingdom of heaven. Those who can accept it should accept it."

Some people brought children to Jesus so that he would place his hands on them and pray. But the disciples scolded them. "Allow the children to come to me," Jesus said. "Don't forbid them, because the kingdom of heaven belongs to people like these children." Then he blessed the children and went away from there.

REFLECT

These two short moments, back to back in the Gospel of Matthew, take a bit of digging into to really understand. Let's start with eunuchs. In the ancient world there were people who were called eunuchs. Often, they were men who, in the course of war, had their genitals injured (sometimes on purpose by the people capturing them). In a world that cared a lot about binaries—things and people being one thing or another with nothing in between—these people were left out of a lot of the public life. They occupied a third-gendered space, not considered men anymore, but also not considered women. There are parts of the Hebrew Scriptures that exclude eunuchs, while other parts of the Hebrew Scriptures paint them as heroes (like in the book of Esther) or promise them a name greater than sons or daughters (like in Isaiah). We don't entirely know how eunuchs felt about themselves, or how they would have described their gender, but today many intersex people and transgender people look to the eunuchs as ancestors in experience.

CONNECT HEAD AND HEART

> **Who are some people in today's world that are overlooked or pushed to the side?**

> **Are there people in your life who treat your ideas and opinions with respect? How does that make you feel?**

> **What do you think our world would look like if the people with the least amount of power were the ones making decisions? How would things be different?**

Jesus talks about eunuchs only once that we know of and it's recorded here. He talks about three different kinds of eunuchs: those who were born that way (so maybe intersex folks), those who were made that way (so probably people who were injured in war), and those who chose to make themselves eunuchs for the sake of heaven. No one really knows what Jesus meant by that last part. But also, sometimes there is bias even in scholarly work when people doing the interpreting don't want to accept a possible interpretation because it makes them uncomfortable. This is why when we read passages like this we have to read LOTS of interpretations and make sure to read interpretations by people who are on the margins (like Black, womanist, feminist, and LGBTQ+ scholars). We need all of our thinking together in order to really understand how to live out our faith in the world.

Throughout his ministry Jesus emphasized that those with the least power, those who were pushed to the outside, those who were considered worthless by the majority, were the ones who God prioritized and cared most about.

Whatever Jesus meant by these three groups of eunuchs, what is clear is that he was telling those listening that eunuchs were to be accepted and welcomed into the community. They weren't asked to change or stop being eunuchs, they were simply welcomed.

And it's not a coincidence that the next story in this short passage is about another group of people who, in Jesus' time, didn't have a lot of protections. Children in the ancient world weren't treated the same way children are today. They were seen as the property of their parents, considered part of the household that had to give total allegiance to the (male) head of the household. Which included working, if that's what the householder wanted. Children were property, at the mercy of the adults in their world.

When some people brought children to Jesus, his disciples tried to push them away. They considered the children not worth Jesus' time. They were beneath him. But instead of agreeing with his followers, Jesus corrects them and welcomes the children. He also says, "The kingdom of heaven belongs to people like these children." What did he mean by that?

Throughout his ministry Jesus emphasized that those with the least power, those who were pushed to the outside, those who were considered worthless by the majority, were the ones who God prioritized and cared most about. Saying that the kingdom of heaven belongs to children means that God's priorities are different to the priorities of the world. People prioritize power and money. God prioritizes children and the weak.

CONNECT HEART AND HANDS

- **Find someone younger than you and do something special for them. How did it make you feel and what did you learn?**
- **Ask someone younger than you to teach you something. Again, how did it make you feel and what did you learn?**

Jesus was saying that if you want to be close to God, be close to the people who have no power. Listen to them and learn from them. Center them and their needs. Work to create systems and policies that protect the most vulnerable. Do what you can to take care of those who need help and support.

Following Jesus means focusing on the same people he did. Imagine how different our world would be if everyone was focused on making sure that those who had the least were taken care of, on making sure that children had a voice?

QUESTIONING JESUS

Matthew 19:16–30

READ

A man approached him and said, "Teacher, what good thing must I do to have eternal life?"

Jesus said, "Why do you ask me about what is good? There's only one who is good. If you want to enter eternal life, keep the commandments."

The man said, "Which ones?"

Then Jesus said, *"Don't commit murder. Don't commit adultery. Don't steal. Don't give false testimony. Honor your father and mother, and love your neighbor as you love yourself."*

The young man replied, "I've kept all these. What am I still missing?"

Jesus said, "If you want to be complete, go, sell what you own, and give the money to the poor. Then you will have treasure in heaven. And come follow me."

But when the young man heard this, he went away saddened, because he had many possessions.

Then Jesus said to his disciples, "I assure you that it will be very hard for a rich person to enter the kingdom of heaven. In fact, it's easier for a camel to squeeze through the eye of a needle than for a rich person to enter God's kingdom."

When his disciples heard this, they were stunned. "Then who can be saved?" they asked.

CONNECT HEAD AND HEART

> Why do you think the rich man went away sad?

> Do you think the rich man later changed his mind and came back?

> Why do you think Jesus said it would be hard for a rich person to enter into God's kingdom?

> What are some things it would be really hard for you to give up to follow Jesus?

Jesus looked at them carefully and said, "It's impossible for human beings. But all things are possible for God."

Then Peter replied, "Look, we've left everything and followed you. What will we have?"

Jesus said to them, "I assure you who have followed me that, when everything is made new, when the Human One sits on his magnificent throne, you also will sit on twelve thrones overseeing the twelve tribes of Israel. And all who have left houses, brothers, sisters, father, mother, children, or farms because of my name will receive one hundred times more and will inherit eternal life. But many who are first will be last. And many who are last will be first.

REFLECT

As Jesus was gaining more popularity as a teacher he had two main audiences. One was the people who had given up everything to follow Jesus and join in his movement (often called the disciples); Jesus spends more time with them and offers them separate teachings. The other group was people who were curious about Jesus, who had heard some of his public talks or seen his incredible deeds, but who weren't ready to fully commit yet.

We see the overlap of both of these audiences in today's story. A man, someone who was curious about Jesus, comes up to him while he is gathered with his inner circle. This man asks Jesus what he has to do to inherit eternal life. It's an honest question. This man wants to do the right thing. Jesus first tells him to obey the most important Jewish laws; he lists laws from the Ten Commandments and from the Levitical laws, ones that any faithful Jewish person would know and live by. The man says he's done all of that since he was young but he still senses something is missing. There is something more he needs to do.

Jesus is saying the rules of right relationship are important and you can't really be in right relationship with other people if you're not doing justice.

Jesus answers, "Sell what you own, and give the money to the poor."

Wow. That's a tough one. The man's response is striking: "He went away saddened, because he had many possessions."

Now, lots of people have debated this story over the years. Did Jesus REALLY mean that you have to give away everything you have? Folks who are uncomfortable with this story often say you just have to be WILLING to give it all away, you don't actually have to do it.

Jesus goes on to teach his inner circle more about what he means: "It's easier for a camel to squeeze through the eye of a needle than for a rich person to enter God's kingdom." Peter, one of the people closest to Jesus, is upset by this: "Then who can be saved?" And I think there we have something really important to pay attention to.

CONNECT HEART AND HANDS

- **Find a documentary or an interview about someone who experienced a lot of poverty. What do you learn from their experiences?**
- **Experiment with giving something up in order to spend more time working for justice. Maybe you take a couple of weeks or a month off social media. Maybe you commit to not buying anything new for a while and giving your allowance to an organization working on a cause you care about. Maybe you give away or donate some things to someone else who might need them. Then reflect on the experience.**

Jesus was living in a world that, in some ways, was not so different from ours. People with a lot of wealth are able to provide a really nice life for themselves. They can afford expensive healthcare, healthy food, safe houses, clean water, the list goes on. People without a lot of money often suffer, from housing insecurity, from a lack of healthcare, from an inability to eat healthy food or have clean water.

Sometimes, with the way our systems are set up, it can seem like the people with money are somehow more righteous, when really it's just that they have more access to what they need.

And sometimes, when you have access, when you can buy whatever you want and need, you can also start to think that you don't need help or community. You don't need the support of others. You can be kind or give a little bit to charity, but you're not really invested in your neighborhood or community because you don't have to be.

I think one of the things Jesus is highlighting with this story is that for those who have a lot it is much harder to join the Jesus movement because you might be unaware or unwilling to do what you need to do for the world to be more just. You can feel like if you just play by the rules you'll continue to be able to get whatever you want and need.

Jesus is saying the rules of right relationship are important and you can't really be in right relationship with other people if you're not doing justice.

Jesus then goes on to tell his friends that anyone who has given something up will get it back, and I think what he's getting at is you might suffer for a little while, you might be a little uncomfortable, but justice is better for everyone. Community is better for everyone. When you really invest in following in the way of Jesus, when you show up for your neighbors, when you work for justice, when you share what you have, everything will be better, for you and the people around you. And THAT is what the kingdom of God looks like.

THE SHEEP AND THE GOATS

Matthew 25:31–46

READ

"Now when the Human One comes in his majesty and all his angels are with him, he will sit on his majestic throne. All the nations will be gathered in front of him. He will separate them from each other, just as a shepherd separates the sheep from the goats. He will put the sheep on his right side. But the goats he will put on his left.

"Then the king will say to those on his right, 'Come, you who will receive good things from my Father. Inherit the kingdom that was prepared for you before the world began. I was hungry and you gave me food to eat. I was thirsty and you gave me a drink. I was a stranger and you welcomed me. I was naked and you gave me clothes to wear. I was sick and you took care of me. I was in prison and you visited me.'

"Then those who are righteous will reply to him, 'Lord, when did we see you hungry and feed you, or thirsty and give you a drink? When did we see you as a stranger and welcome you, or naked and give you clothes to wear? When did we see you sick or in prison and visit you?'

"Then the king will reply to them, 'I assure you that when you have done it for one of the least of these brothers and sisters of mine, you have done it for me.'

CONNECT HEAD AND HEART

> Who are the people our world considers as the "least of these"?

> What other messages do you find in Jesus' story about the sheep and the goats?

> What are some ways that you could work to see the image of Jesus in other people?

"Then he will say to those on his left, 'Get away from me, you who will receive terrible things. Go into the unending fire that has been prepared for the devil and his angels. I was hungry and you didn't give me food to eat. I was thirsty and you didn't give me anything to drink. I was a stranger and you didn't welcome me. I was naked and you didn't give me clothes to wear. I was sick and in prison, and you didn't visit me.'

"Then they will reply, 'Lord, when did we see you hungry or thirsty or a stranger or naked or sick or in prison and didn't do anything to help you?' Then he will answer, 'I assure you that when you haven't done it for one of the least of these, you haven't done it for me.' And they will go away into eternal punishment. But the righteous ones will go into eternal life."

REFLECT

Jesus often taught using something called a "parable." A parable is a story with a deeper meaning behind it meant to teach a lesson on how to behave. It's kind of like the original Grimm's *Fairy Tales* which taught children lessons about scary things. These stories aren't necessarily meant to be taken as true things that actually happened (or that will happen) but as a way to help explain the kind of things Jesus wanted his followers to do. The story you just read is one of those parables. It's part of a series of stories Jesus tells about being ready. In Jesus' time there were a lot of people who thought the world was going to come to an end and they needed to be ready. It was a scary time and people were looking for some kind of assurance. There were some people who said that only the ones who believed like they did would be saved if something happened. And in the midst of that Jesus tells this story.

That's what it means to be in right relationship with other people. That's how we honor the work Jesus did and the person Jesus was.

It can kind of seem like a scary story—separation and being sent to eternal punishment—but what happens if we look at the story UNDER the story?

Jesus is telling a story about a group of people who ignore everyone who's hurting. They don't pay any attention to people who need clothing, or who are in prison for a long time, or who are hungry and thirsty. They ignore the people who really need a friend, but then they claim to be doing all of the right things!

Meanwhile, there's another group who are quietly taking care of everyone, not because they want to win points or get rewards but because they know it's the right thing to do. Jesus tells them this is the right behavior. Not only that, but every time they have cared for one of the "least of these" they've been caring for God.

CONNECT HEART AND HANDS

- **Volunteer with your friends and/or family to feed people who are hungry.**
- **Get involved with your local prison book project, donating books to people who are incarcerated and letting them know they aren't forgotten.**
- **Support organizations that work to provide clean water to people in your own country and around the world.**

Jesus is telling us that the image of God is found in the people who are often ignored and that the best way to serve God is to pay attention to the people the world considers the "least of these." To be friends with people who are lonely. To make sure people have enough food to eat and clean water to drink. To give people clothing. To visit (or write letters) to people in prison so they know they are not forgotten.

That's what it means to be in right relationship with other people. That's how we honor the work Jesus did and the person Jesus was.

JESUS' INVITATION

Mark 1:16–20

READ

As Jesus passed alongside the Galilee Sea, he saw two brothers, Simon and Andrew, throwing fishing nets into the sea, for they were fishermen. "Come, follow me," he said, "and I'll show you how to fish for people." Right away, they left their nets and followed him. After going a little farther, he saw James and John, Zebedee's sons, in their boat repairing the fishing nets. At that very moment he called them. They followed him, leaving their father Zebedee in the boat with the hired workers.

REFLECT

The Gospel of Mark doesn't start out with Jesus' birth story or any stories about him as a kid or teenager. Instead, we are put right into the action with adult Jesus starting his public ministry. Almost right away he begins calling people to follow him, to join him in his public work.

The first people he calls are all men who worked catching fish. In the Hebrew Scriptures, the image of "fishing" or "hooking fish" was used to talk about how God would handle people who exploited others. God would send people with hooks to remove the offenders. In Amos 4:2 it says: "The Lord God has solemnly promised by his holiness: The days are surely coming upon you, when they will take you away with hooks, even the last one of you with fishhooks."

CONNECT HEAD AND HEART

> **What do you think Simon, Andrew, James, and John were feeling as they left everything to follow Jesus?**
>
> **Do you think it was harder for James and John because they were leaving their family behind?**
>
> **Why do you think Jesus called these particular people?**
>
> **Do you think there were some people Jesus called who refused his invitation?**
>
> **What kind of invitation would be so captivating to you that you'd drop everything to follow the person who offered it?**

Simon and Andrew, James and John would have known these Scriptures, and as they stood there with their own fishing gear, spending their time and energy making wealth for the people who oppressed them, they would have understood in a profound way that as Jesus is calling them to "fish for people," he is calling them to be part of significant change – standing up for those who are being exploited.

Jesus isn't calling these men to just be missionaries, or to tell people about the work Jesus is doing, he is calling them to be a part of a new movement, one where the old ways are set aside and people order themselves in a different way.

Jesus calls them to leave the security of their jobs, the security of their extended family, and to be a part of a new movement that is working to bring attention to the injustice of the current age and work for a more just way of being a community.

This invitation was so exciting to these men that they dropped everything instantly to follow! I think part of what made it easier for them is they might have believed they had nothing to lose. Things were so dire, they faced so much oppression, the work they had wasn't enough to make ends meet, and they looked around and saw how bad things were and were ready to do whatever it took to usher in a new world. They were ready to give up family and a familiar way of life to follow Jesus.

As we think about our lives today, do we still see the call of Jesus as that exciting? Does it feel so compelling that we'd be willing to give up comfort and safety in order to do what Jesus is asking of us? And if not, might that be because we're not understanding what God really wants us to do?

CONNECT HEART AND HANDS

- Take a look at a variety of church websites. What kind of invitations do they offer to people? Do you find those invitations compelling? Write out a new message that you DO find compelling.
- Craft an invitation to someone else to join you in work that you're passionate about (maybe it's a volunteer opportunity or a justice issue you care about). Think really hard about what would make this invitation compelling to the OTHER person.

As we think about our lives today, do we still see the call of Jesus as that exciting? Does it feel so compelling that we'd be willing to give up comfort and safety in order to do what Jesus is asking of us? And if not, might that be because we're not understanding what God really wants us to do?

If we imagine the call of God to follow Jesus as something that offers us everything we've dreamed of, how might that change how we feel about following Jesus?

LEVI'S STORY

Mark 2:13–17

READ

Jesus went out beside the lake again. The whole crowd came to him, and he began to teach them. As he continued along, he saw Levi, Alphaeus' son, sitting at a kiosk for collecting taxes. Jesus said to him, "Follow me." Levi got up and followed him.

Jesus sat down to eat at Levi's house. Many tax collectors and sinners were eating with Jesus and his disciples. Indeed, many of them had become his followers. When some of the legal experts from among the Pharisees saw that he was eating with sinners and tax collectors, they asked his disciples, "Why is he eating with sinners and tax collectors?"

When Jesus heard it, he said to them, "Healthy people don't need a doctor, but sick people do. I didn't come to call righteous people, but sinners."

REFLECT

In our story today Jesus is still early in his public ministry. He's still gathering people to him and inviting them to be his followers. As we've talked about in other places, this invitation wasn't just about religious ideas and ideals; it was an invitation to be a part of changing the society they lived in to be more just and more like what God wants.

We can imagine there were certain people who were especially attracted to this invitation: people who didn't have very much money, people who were very aware of how unfair the world they lived in was, people without a lot of privilege or power. The people with nothing to lose, basically.

CONNECT HEAD AND HEART

> Why do you think the religious leaders were upset with Jesus for eating with tax collectors and sinners?

> What do you think it would have felt like to be Levi and be called by Jesus?

> If Jesus were preaching and teaching on earth today, what kinds of people do you think he would call to be his followers?

> Can you think of some things that benefit one group of people but do harm to another group?

But then there were people like Levi. Levi was a tax collector. In that time tax collectors were considered to be traitors. They were acting in co-operation with the Roman authorities and taking money away from their own people.

Many tax collectors took more than they were required to, padding their own pockets at the expense of their neighbors. Needless to say, not a lot of folks liked tax collectors!

So we can understand why the religious leaders, the people called Pharisees, were upset that not only was Jesus teaching tax collectors but that he was eating in their homes and inviting them to join his movement. The Pharisees' response maybe sounds judgmental to us today, but when we understand the context we can see why they had a right to be upset! Jesus was eating with traitors! He was inviting people who were taking advantage of their neighbors to be a part of his new movement!

They question Jesus about it and he was ready with a response: "Healthy people don't need a doctor, but sick people do. I didn't come to call righteous people, but sinners." Jesus is saying, look, these are the people who need to change if we're going to have a new way of being in community with one another. If we're going to have justice, the tax collectors are going to have to stop taking more than they're supposed to (and maybe will need to quit their jobs altogether).

Jesus offers compassion for folks who probably didn't get a lot of compassion. But more than that, he calls them to be better. He gives them a place in the movement. He invites them to change their ways and work for justice.

It's a reminder that everyone has a place in the work of Jesus. Everyone has a place in the kingdom of God. We just have to be willing to participate fully, which means looking out for each other, sharing what we have, not co-operating with systems and structures that oppress others, and being willing to give up things that benefit us but hurt others.

It's a reminder that everyone has a place in the work of Jesus. Everyone has a place in the kingdom of God. We just have to be willing to participate fully, which means looking out for each other, sharing what we have, not co-operating with systems and structures that oppress others, and being willing to give up things that benefit us but hurt others.

Jesus' call to "follow me" still echoes for us today. We are still invited to follow and to be a part of the community working to make things better and more just for everyone.

Sometimes that means examining places where we might have it easier than other people because of things outside of our control (like how much money our family has, the color of our skin, or what country we were born in. This is sometimes called "privilege") and exploring how we can work so that other people who don't share those things can have it easier too.

Sometimes it means accepting grace when we've messed up and making sure we don't make the same mistake again. Sometimes it means confronting the places in our lives where we judge other people and their choices and figuring out how to have compassion for them instead of continuing to judge.

Following Jesus means being centered on those who are on the outskirts and doing whatever we can to make sure they are OK.

CONNECT HEART AND HANDS

- Is there a group of people you are judgmental about? Explore more about them and try to understand them better. Maybe you can read a book about them or watch a documentary or listen to some interviews.
- Is there someone in your school or neighborhood who is often left out? Do something nice for them this week.

JESUS STARTS A NEW TRADITION

Mark 14:12–26

READ

On the first day of the Festival of Unleavened Bread, when the Passover lamb was sacrificed, the disciples said to Jesus, "Where do you want us to prepare for you to eat the Passover meal?"

He sent two of his disciples and said to them, "Go into the city. A man carrying a water jar will meet you. Follow him. Wherever he enters, say to the owner of the house, 'The teacher asks, "Where is my guest room where I can eat the Passover meal with my disciples?"' He will show you a large room upstairs already furnished. Prepare for us there." The disciples left, came into the city, found everything just as he had told them, and they prepared the Passover meal.

That evening, Jesus arrived with the Twelve. During the meal, Jesus said, "I assure you that one of you will betray me—someone eating with me."

Deeply saddened, they asked him, one by one, "It's not me, is it?"

Jesus answered, "It's one of the Twelve, one who is dipping bread with me into this bowl. The Human One goes to his death just as it is written about him. But how terrible it is for that person who betrays the Human One! It would have been better for him if he had never been born."

While they were eating, Jesus took bread, blessed it, broke it, and gave it to them, and said, "Take; this is my body." He took a cup, gave thanks, and gave it to them, and they all drank from it. He said to them, "This is my blood of the covenant, which is poured out for many. I assure you that I won't drink wine again until that day when I drink it in a new way in God's kingdom." After singing songs of praise, they went out to the Mount of Olives.

REFLECT

Today's story takes place in the final week of Jesus' life. He has come to Jerusalem, the seat of religious and political power, to challenge the systems that keep people oppressed and to proclaim that another world is possible. He doesn't live in Jerusalem so he needs to find places to stay and supplies for the work that's ahead. On top of that, it's a special time in the Jewish religious calendar: the celebration of Passover.

Passover is a time when the Jewish people remember that they were once enslaved in Egypt and that God led them to freedom. There are special things they do to commemorate that experience. They share special food together and eat a certain kind of bread; there are prayers and traditions. It's a really important time.

Jesus, at this point, knows that the heat is on and the final steps, the ones that will lead to his arrest and death, are coming. So not only is this Passover meal important

CONNECT HEAD AND HEART

> What do you think this meal would have been like for Jesus? How about for his disciples?

> Have you ever been in a situation where you didn't know how you were going to respond? What happened?

> Does your family have any kind of rituals or traditions around food? Maybe a weekly dinner or a special holiday thing? What is it? How does it make you feel?

> Are you part of a religious community that takes Communion or the Eucharist? What has been your experience of participating? If you haven't yet, might you consider it?

spiritually, it's also important personally to Jesus. He knows it might be the last meal he gets to share with the people who he's been traveling with, ministering to and with, and is entrusting the ongoing mission to.

In order to find a place to hold this special meal, Jesus tells his disciples to look for "a man carrying a water jar" and that person would show them to a room. (As a fun side note, this would have been out of character because in Jesus' time carrying water was a job that was mostly done by women. We see here that there are all sorts of people in the Bible breaking down gender norms and barriers!)

The disciples prepare the meal and they eat it together. In this version of the story, there is a kind of sadness to the air. Jesus starts the meal by telling his disciples, his friends, that one of them will betray him. He seems a little angry.

This can be a hard passage to read, but I think it shows us that Jesus has big emotions too. Jesus, too, was hurt, got upset, was frustrated, felt deeply when he knew he was going to be betrayed.

The disciples also had a lot of feelings. They all wondered if they were going to be the one to betray him. On the surface that sounds kind of silly—how could they not know? But in the midst of scary situations we don't always know how we'll react. If they were forced to choose between Jesus and their own safety, what would they choose? It can be hard to know ahead of time. We hope we'll make the right decision but we're not always sure we will.

After this moment, during the meal, Jesus shares bread and wine with his friends, and in the midst of this starts a new tradition, one that many Christians still observe to this day: the tradition of Communion or the Eucharist. It's a reminder of Jesus' life and death.

This ritual was a way for Jesus to mark this moment with his friends. To give them something they could do, even after he wasn't with them anymore, to help them feel connected, to remember his life, and to connect their continued work to everything he had taught them.

CONNECT HEART AND HANDS

- Ask some friends or other religious leaders (or do some research online) about different churches beliefs around Communion. How does this make you think about Communion in new ways?
- Ask your family or friends to have a special meal together. Maybe include something special: a note at each place saying what you appreciate about that person, a picture you drew for them, etc. During the meal spend some time asking one another questions to get to know each other on a deeper level. (Then journal about the experience.)

This ritual was a way for Jesus to mark this moment with his friends. To give them something they could do, even after he wasn't with them anymore, to help them feel connected, to remember his life, and to connect their continued work to everything he had taught them.

We continue to practice this to remind us as well. Of how we are a part of his ongoing legacy and work in the world, that we are connected to him, even all of these years later. What a beautiful thing!

ANGELS AND SHEPHERDS

Luke 2:8–20

READ

Nearby shepherds were living in the fields, guarding their sheep at night. The Lord's angel stood before them, the Lord's glory shone around them, and they were terrified.

The angel said, "Don't be afraid! Look! I bring good news to you—wonderful, joyous news for all people. Your savior is born today in David's city. He is Christ the Lord. This is a sign for you: you will find a newborn baby wrapped snugly and lying in a manger." Suddenly a great assembly of the heavenly forces was with the angel praising God. They said, "Glory to God in heaven, and on earth peace among those whom he favors."

When the angels returned to heaven, the shepherds said to each other, "Let's go right now to Bethlehem and see what's happened. Let's confirm what the Lord has revealed to us." They went quickly and found Mary and Joseph, and the baby lying in the manger. When they saw this, they reported what they had been told about this child. Everyone who heard it was amazed at what the shepherds told them. Mary committed these things to memory and considered them carefully. The shepherds returned home, glorifying and praising God for all they had heard and seen. Everything happened just as they had been told.

REFLECT

You might have heard this story before. It's a popular one. You might have even been a part of acting it out in church as a child! But you might not know all of the juicy details!

When Jesus was born, shepherds weren't very popular. People didn't like them. They thought they were smelly and weird and often didn't want them in their towns or their communities. Shepherds were people you couldn't trust. They hung out alone. They took care of sheep out in the wild places. They were odd.

CONNECT HEAD AND HEART

- Have you ever been afraid about a situation but it turned out to be really good news? What happened?
- What do you think you would do if an angel came to you?
- When you've gotten good news, how did you tell other people about it?
- Can you think of some people in today's world whose word wouldn't be trusted? What might be different if people listened to what they had to say?

Shepherds were not the people you'd tell something important to. They were not the ones you wanted to give an important job to. Shepherds were either overlooked or looked down on.

And yet! In the story the writer of Luke tells us about Jesus' birth; the shepherds are the ones the angel comes to. They get to be the very first people to hear about the good news of Jesus being born!

For those of us who might be unpopular, or feeling weird in our bodies, or dealing with acne and body odor, or feeling overlooked and unheard, this is a reminder that God cares about us and has special work that only we can do.

The news of the birth of Jesus didn't come to people with a lot of money. It didn't go to the king. It didn't go to religious leaders or politicians. It went to the shepherds. In this story not only were they the first people to hear the news, they were also given the job of telling other people about what they had seen! Wow, what a cool thing!

Right from the beginning of this story, the writer is telling us that God is doing something different. God isn't just concerned with the popular and the powerful, the rich and the important; God cares about the weird and odd people, the smelly ones and the ones no one else trusts. Not only that, God has a special mission for them. Throughout this Gospel we'll see this same theme over and over again: God coming to the people who everyone else overlooks.

For those of us who might be unpopular, or feeling weird in our bodies, or dealing with acne and body odor, or feeling overlooked and unheard, this is a reminder that God cares about us and has special work that only we can do.

And it's also a reminder to the people who are popular or have power to not overlook the unpopular people, or the ones on the outside. Instead, we need to look to them for the wisdom and insight only they can provide.

We all have worth. We all have something special to contribute. We need each other.

CONNECT HEART AND HANDS

- **Is there someone you know who's feeling a little lonely or doesn't have a lot of friends? Reach out to say hello and tell them something you appreciate about them.**
- **Are you feeling self-conscious about something in your life? Put a note on your bathroom mirror that says: "God cares about me and has work only I can do!" Look at that note every time you look in the mirror.**
- **Search for positive stories in the news and share them with other people. Who's doing really cool work that's helping other people? Don't just look for super big things, look for small things too.**

JESUS GETS LOST

Luke 2:41–52

READ

Each year [Jesus'] parents went to Jerusalem for the Passover Festival. When he was 12 years old, they went up to Jerusalem according to their custom. After the festival was over, they were returning home, but the boy Jesus stayed behind in Jerusalem. His parents didn't know it. Supposing that he was among their band of travelers, they journeyed on for a full day while looking for him among their family and friends. When they didn't find Jesus, they returned to Jerusalem to look for him. After three days they found him in the temple. He was sitting among the teachers, listening to them and putting questions to them. Everyone who heard him was amazed by his understanding and his answers. When his parents saw him, they were shocked.

His mother said, "Child, why have you treated us like this? Listen! Your father and I have been worried. We've been looking for you!"

Jesus replied, "Why were you looking for me? Didn't you know that it was necessary for me to be in my Father's house?" But they didn't understand what he said to them.

Jesus went down to Nazareth with them and was obedient to them. His mother cherished every word in her heart. Jesus matured in wisdom and years, and in favor with God and with people.

REFLECT

We don't have very many stories from Jesus' childhood.

In this story from Luke, Jesus travels with his parents and extended family to Jerusalem to celebrate Passover, an important religious holiday that helps the Jewish people remember when they were freed from slavery in Egypt. In those days, while the temple was still standing, you would travel to Jerusalem to celebrate the festival.

CONNECT HEAD AND HEART

> **What do you think it would have been like to be Jesus growing up? What do you think it would have been like to be Jesus' parents?**
>
> **Why do you think Jesus found himself drawn to the temple?**
>
> **Have you ever been lost or got separated from your parents/adults? How did you feel? How did your adults react when they found you again?**
>
> **What are the ways you are working to grow in your faith? Who are you learning from?**

After the festival was over the family started to go back home, but Jesus stayed behind. Since they were in a large group, his parents didn't notice he wasn't with them. Maybe they thought he was hanging out with his cousins or other kids his age. But when they'd traveled for a full day and realized they hadn't seen him they started to get worried. They searched the company of people they were with and didn't find him. So they went back to Jerusalem. The writer tells us that they found him after three days.

If Jesus needed to spend time learning and growing, then we definitely need to as well!

They must have been so scared! Three days searching for their child, not knowing if he was safe, not knowing where he was! Then they found him, sitting calmly in the temple, without a care in the world!

Not only was he in the temple, he was with the religious leaders, learning from them and asking them questions that showed how much he knew and how mature his faith was already.

His parents were shocked by all of this, and his mother says what any parent would say: "Child, why have you treated us like this? Listen! Your father and I have been worried. We've been looking for you!"

How many of us have heard the same? "You scared me!" "Where were you?" "Didn't you hear me calling you?" The adults in our lives were worried and scared. When they realize that we're unharmed they get upset that we've caused them to be afraid.

Jesus answers in a rather strange way: "Why were you looking for me? Didn't you know that it was necessary for me to be in my Father's house?" This is especially telling because his mother had just said, "Your father and I have been worried." But Jesus turns around and says he's in his Father's house. The story tells us his parents didn't understand what he was saying.

CONNECT HEART AND HANDS

- **Thinking about Jesus growing in wisdom, what is one thing in your faith that you can work on to grow this week?**
- **Spend some time with other religious people this week. Go to a church service or prayer service, serve with other people who are religious, pray or worship with others.**

The writer of Luke is trying to let his readers know that Jesus feels connected to God in a way that other people don't understand. He feels drawn to being with the religious leaders in the temple, learning all that he can. He feels connected to this place of worship, a unique place in his religious tradition where God dwells and the people can connect with God. Luke is telling us that Jesus is special and that he was special from a young age.

The story goes on to say that Jesus returned home with his parents and was obedient to them. He grew in wisdom. He also grew in favor with God and with other people.

Jesus might have had an early connection to God and been wise beyond his years, but he also had to grow up and figure out how to live in this world. He had to be formed and shaped in his relationships to God and to other people. He had to learn and grow.

And he knew that some of that learning and growing needed to happen with religious leaders who could answer his questions and help him think more deeply about his faith.

If Jesus needed to spend time learning and growing, then we definitely need to as well! We can seek out people who can help us to think about our faith and how to grow in wisdom. We can seek out experiences that will help us to live out our faith and put it into practice in the world. We can seek out community to help us live out our values.

We, too, can grow in wisdom and in favor with God and other people.

JESUS ON A MISSION

Luke 4:14–22

READ

Jesus returned in the power of the Spirit to Galilee, and news about him spread throughout the whole countryside. He taught in their synagogues and was praised by everyone.

Jesus went to Nazareth, where he had been raised. On the Sabbath he went to the synagogue as he normally did and stood up to read. The synagogue assistant gave him the scroll from the prophet Isaiah. He unrolled the scroll and found the place where it was written:

The Spirit of the Lord is upon me,
because the Lord has anointed me.
He has sent me to preach good news to the poor,
to proclaim release to the prisoners
and recovery of sight to the blind,
to liberate the oppressed,
and to proclaim the year of the Lord's favor.

He rolled up the scroll, gave it back to the synagogue assistant, and sat down. Every eye in the synagogue was fixed on him. He began to explain to them, "Today, this scripture has been fulfilled just as you heard it."

REFLECT

After Jesus was baptized, after he spent time in the wilderness, he begins to teach and travel around. As word about him spreads, he decides to go back to the town where he was raised. He goes to the synagogue, the place where Jewish folks gathered to learn and pray. The passage tells us this is something he did regularly, it was part of his religious practice. He spent time in community. He observed religious traditions and rituals.

CONNECT HEAD AND HEART

- **What religious traditions and rituals do you (and/or your family) observe?**
- **Which of these traditions are the most meaningful to you?**
- **What are some traditions you might want to try?**
- **What are some things you dream about for the world?**
- **What are some things you see in your area that you think could be improved?**

At this particular service, the reading from the holy Scriptures is from the prophet Isaiah. Jesus reads: "The Spirit of the Lord is upon me, because the Lord has anointed me. He has sent me to preach good news to the poor, to proclaim release to the prisoners and recovery of sight to the blind, to liberate the oppressed, and to proclaim the year of the Lord's favor."

Jesus takes this passage as the mission statement for

his work and ministry. He declares himself as one who is picking up the mantle of Isaiah and continuing that work.

His mission is to do five things:

1. Preach good news to the poor.
2. Proclaim release to the prisoners.
3. Recovery of sight to the blind.
4. To liberate the oppressed.
5. To proclaim the year of the Lord's favor.

All of these things are centered on justice and community. Jesus is saying that he wants people to know that God cares about your physical needs as well as your spiritual needs. God wants to make sure that people have enough food to eat and a safe place to live. God wants us to think

These are bold ideas. We might read them even today and struggle with them. Are they even possible? What would a world like that look like? How could we make this happen? It brings up fears in us. Doubts. We wonder if it's even possible.

about how we can set prisoners free, which also means creating a community where people can be safe. God wants people to have healthcare and to be able to access resources and community, no matter their disability. God wants the oppressed to be liberated. And God wants the year of the Lord's favor, also called "Jubilee," which was a practice where every fifty years all debts would be forgiven and land was returned to its original owners. It was a way to make sure that even if someone fell on hard times they wouldn't be that way forever, nor would they pass that down to their children or grandchildren.

CONNECT HEART AND HANDS

- **Find a new spiritual practice and give it a try. Maybe go somewhere and walk a labyrinth, or learn how to pray with beads, or try to use a different prayer book than you usually do. You could make a prayer journal and decorate it. Try the practice for at least a week and reflect on how it feels.**
- **Take one of the things that you thought could be improved in your area and do some research to see if anyone is working on it and if you can get involved.**
- **What's one thing you could do this week to make the world around you a better place?**

These are bold ideas. We might read them even today and struggle with them. Are they even possible? What would a world like that look like? How could we make this happen? It brings up fears in us. Doubts. We wonder if it's even possible.

People in Jesus' time wondered the same. It seemed unbelievable that any of it could be true. They were under Roman occupation, they were struggling, the divide between people who had money and those who didn't was getting wider and wider. It was easy to look around and think nothing could be changed.

If you were listening to Jesus' message and you were poor, or oppressed, or blind, or in prison it could also be easy to feel like you didn't have any power to change things. Everyone around you was too powerful and there was nothing you could do.

You might feel that way now: you're too young, you don't have money, you can't do anything.

But over and over again, Jesus tells people to do what they can where they are. To start small. To do something to work for justice. Which means we can be a part of that work too. Starting from wherever we are with whatever skills, talents, ability, and access we have.

THE GOOD BAD GUY

Luke 10:25–37

READ

A legal expert stood up to test Jesus. "Teacher," he said, "what must I do to gain eternal life?"

Jesus replied, "What is written in the Law? How do you interpret it?"

He responded, "*You must love the Lord your God with all your heart, with all your being, with all your strength, and with all your mind, and love your neighbor as yourself.*"

Jesus said to him, "You have answered correctly. Do this and you will live."

But the legal expert wanted to prove that he was right, so he said to Jesus, "And who is my neighbor?"

Jesus replied, "A man went down from Jerusalem to Jericho. He encountered thieves, who stripped him naked, beat him up, and left him near death. Now it just so happened that a priest was also going down the same road. When he saw the injured man, he crossed over to the other side of the road and went on his way. Likewise, a Levite came by that spot, saw the injured man, and crossed over to the other side of the road and went on his way. A

Samaritan, who was on a journey, came to where the man was. But when he saw him, he was moved with compassion. The Samaritan went to him and bandaged his wounds, tending them with oil and wine. Then he placed the wounded man on his own donkey, took him to an inn, and took care of him. The next day, he took two full days' worth of wages and gave them to the innkeeper. He said, 'Take care of him, and when I return, I will pay you back for any additional costs.' What do you think? Which one of these three was a neighbor to the man who encountered thieves?"

CONNECT HEAD AND HEART

> Why do you think Jesus used a story to answer the question he was asked?

> What do you think the people listening would have thought of Jesus' story?

> What does Jesus' story make you think about in your own life?

> Have you ever had someone ask you a question and it felt like they were trying to trick you? How did you feel? How did you respond?

> How might you work to look out for your neighbors?

Then the legal expert said, "The one who demonstrated mercy toward him."

Jesus told him, "Go and do likewise."

REFLECT

As Jesus traveled around teaching people, sometimes folks came to him with questions. Every once in a while these questions seemed to come from a place of wanting to trick or trap Jesus, to get him to say something that would get him in trouble with the political authorities or get the crowds to turn against him. Or sometimes the questions were about not wanting to accept Jesus' answer.

In our text today we have someone who is very well-versed in the Jewish religious law who comes to Jesus to ask him a question. Jesus, at first, answers the question plainly and he tells this expert what the law says: "You must love the Lord your God with all your heart, with all your being, with all your strength, and with all your mind, and love your neighbor as yourself."

Jesus uses this story to challenge the ideas of those listening and to expand their notions of who their neighbor is. It's not just about what you say, or what status you hold, it's about what you do. It's about looking out for people who need help.

But the legal expert isn't satisfied. He wants Jesus' answer to be more clearly defined, or to let him off the hook, and so he asks, "Who is my neighbor?" Jesus decides, this time, to tell him a story.

In the story a man is attacked and robbed. He's left on the side of the road. The first two people who come along, a priest and a Levite, are people who would have been considered good and holy. They are religious, they are supposed to care about others, they are the ones that you would expect to help this injured person! And yet they not only don't stop and help, they cross to the other side of the road to avoid any contact at all.

CONNECT HEART AND HANDS

- **Rewrite Jesus' story to put it in a modern setting. Share it with someone.**
- **Think about a type of person or a community that you might initially judge or have negative feelings about. Do some research to learn more about what that person or community faces and what they are like and see how it changes your initial opinion.**

The third person to come along is a Samaritan. This is a person from the area of Samaria and there was a long and complicated history between Jewish people and Samaritans; there was a longstanding hatred between these two communities. For Jesus to talk about a Samaritan would have immediately made the audience think they were going to be the bad guy. Instead, Jesus uses his story to subvert their expectations, to turn their ideas on their heads. Instead of the priest and the Levite, people the audience would have expected to be good, Jesus makes the hero of the story the Samaritan.

The Samaritan not only stops and helps this man but also pays for his care and continues to care for him through his whole recovery. He is generous beyond even what would have been expected.

Now Jesus turns back to the person who asked the question: which one of these people acted like a neighbor? The answer, as much as the questioner might have hated to admit, was clear: it was the Samaritan.

Jesus uses this story to challenge the ideas of those listening and to expand their notions of who their neighbor is. It's not just about what you say, or what status you hold, it's about what you do. It's about looking out for people who need help.

Jesus' story asks us to consider two things. Who are the people who we look down on or discount or don't expect anything good from? We are asked to reconsider making judgments and to look at our own biases and prejudice.

Then Jesus' story asks us to think about how we can look out for our neighbors. Who needs help? Will we offer the help or will we cross to the other side of the street and avoid getting involved? We are asked to be like the Samaritan and to help others, to have an expanded and expansive understanding of who our neighbors are, and to not look away when someone needs our help.

THE RUNAWAY SON

Luke 15:11–32

READ

Jesus said, "A certain man had two sons. The younger son said to his father, 'Father, give me my share of the inheritance.' Then the father divided his estate between them. Soon afterward, the younger son gathered everything together and took a trip to a land far away. There, he wasted his wealth through extravagant living.

"When he had used up his resources, a severe food shortage arose in that country and he began to be in need. He hired himself out to one of the citizens of that country, who sent him into his fields to feed pigs. He longed to eat his fill from what the pigs ate, but no one gave him anything. When he came to his senses, he said, 'How many of my father's hired hands have more than enough food, but I'm starving to death! I will get up and go to my father, and say to him, "Father, I have sinned against heaven and against you. I no longer deserve to be called your son. Take me on as one of your hired hands."' So he got up and went to his father.

"While he was still a long way off, his father saw him and was moved with compassion. His father ran to him, hugged him, and kissed him. Then his son said, 'Father, I have sinned against heaven and against you. I no longer deserve to be called your son.' But the father said to his servants, 'Quickly, bring out the best robe and put it on him! Put a ring on his finger and sandals on his feet! Fetch the fattened calf and slaughter it. We must celebrate with feasting because this son of mine was dead and has come back to life! He was lost and is found!' And they began to celebrate.

"Now his older son was in the field. Coming in from the field, he approached the house and heard music and dancing. He called one of the servants and asked what was going on. The servant replied, 'Your brother has arrived, and your father has slaughtered the fattened calf because he received his son back safe and sound.' Then the older son was furious and didn't want to enter in, but his father came out and begged him. He answered his father, 'Look, I've served you all these years, and I never disobeyed your instruction. Yet you've never given me as much as a young goat so I could celebrate with my friends. But when this son of yours returned, after gobbling up your estate on prostitutes, you slaughtered the fattened calf for him.' Then his father said, 'Son, you are always with me, and everything I have is yours. But we had to celebrate and be glad because this brother of yours was dead and is alive. He was lost and is found.'"

REFLECT

Often as Jesus traveled with his friends and followers, people would ask him questions. Or he would see something and decide it was a moment for teaching. In these moments, instead of giving a sermon or a list of things to do, Jesus often told stories. Sometimes, because of how far removed we are from the time of Jesus, it's hard to understand the stories. But the people who heard them would have immediately gotten the references, the jokes, the irony of Jesus' stories.

CONNECT HEAD AND HEART

- Has there ever been a story you've heard that had a big impact on your life? What was the story? How did it change you?
- Have you ever felt jealous of a sibling or cousin? Why did you feel jealous? What happened?
- What do you think it would have been like for the younger brother to come home. What do you think it would have been like to be the older brother?
- What do you think this story teaches us about God?

In today's reading we have one of Jesus' most famous stories. Often people will call it the "parable of the Prodigal Son." Parable is a word for a story designed to teach or instruct. The prodigal son is what a lot of people call the younger brother in this story, the brother who asked for his inheritance and left home.

On the surface this story seems pretty simple. A younger brother asks for his share of the inheritance, money that would have belonged to him after his father died, and goes off to another city.

He soon runs out of money and finds himself eating scraps designed for animals. So he decides to go home, ask for forgiveness, and see if he can at least work for his father.

But his father has been waiting for him and he welcomes the boy, restores his place as his son, and throws a banquet to celebrate.

Now the older brother is jealous because he's been doing all the right things; he stayed home, he's been working hard, and he wants the same attention his brother is getting. His father tells him, "Everything I have is yours, but we have to celebrate your brother because he was lost and now he's home."

But underneath this seemingly simple story are some other details we might miss.

When the younger brother asks for his share of the inheritance it's a pretty big insult to his father. It's almost as if he's saying, "I wish you were dead."

Jesus is trying to tell us something about God here. The extravagant love of a parent who will watch and wait and welcome back someone who messes up. A parent who will throw a party when the wanderer comes home. A parent who will assure the older brother he, too, is loved.

After he spends his money, the story says "a severe food shortage arose." It wasn't just that he was wasteful (though he was), he was in a place where there wasn't enough to go around. In his own community there would have been people to look out for him. He would have been known, there would have been people to share their food with him. But now he's in a place where he is not known. No one was willing to share or help him out.

And so he ends up working with pigs. In the Jewish culture pigs are considered unclean. Jesus' audience would have understood how far this young person had fallen. He was desperate enough to work with something his entire culture considered unclean, and not only that, to eat the food the pigs wouldn't even eat! It's a pretty terrible situation to be in.

So he goes back home intending to be a servant. And yet the father not only welcomes him back but spots him way down the road, which meant that this father was expecting his son to return. The father didn't write off the son, he didn't banish him, he didn't consider him dead (even though he might have been justified to do so). He waited and watched. When he saw his son he ran and greeted him and didn't even consider his proposal for a second. He just reinstated him as his son.

We can understand why the older brother was angry. He did everything right. He stayed. He was faithful. To see his brother celebrated made him jealous and angry. How many of us have been in the same position? Where a sibling gets more attention than we do? Or we put in all of the work on a group project but then don't get the credit? It can be hard to feel overlooked.

The father reminds the older brother that his place is secure. It's always been secure, but his younger brother needs to be welcomed back. He needs to be restored. He needs to know he is forgiven.

Jesus is trying to tell us something about God here. The extravagant love of a parent who will watch and wait and welcome back someone who messes up. A parent who will throw a party when the wanderer comes home. A parent who will assure the older brother he, too, is loved.

CONNECT HEART AND HANDS

- **Find an organization in your community that supports people who are in recovery or re-entering society after being incarcerated. See if there is anything you can do to support their work.**
- **Do something nice for someone in your class who often feels left out.**
- **Write your own version of this story and share it with a friend.**

This story is also a reminder to us to treat one another with kindness and love. To give people second chances (when we can) and to welcome them back into the community. To remember that in the love of God there is always enough to go around. And we can be assured that we, too, are loved and have a place in the household of God.

COME AND SEE

John 1:35–42

READ

The next day John was standing again with two of his disciples. When he saw Jesus walking along he said, "Look! The Lamb of God!" The two disciples heard what he said, and they followed Jesus.

When Jesus turned and saw them following, he asked, "What are you looking for?"

They said, "Rabbi (which is translated *Teacher*), where are you staying?"

He replied, "Come and see." So they went and saw where he was staying, and they remained with him that day. It was about four o'clock in the afternoon.

One of the two disciples who heard what John said and followed Jesus was Andrew, the brother of Simon Peter. He first found his own brother Simon and said to him, "We have found the Messiah" (which is translated *Christ*). He led him to Jesus.

Jesus looked at him and said, "You are Simon, son of John. You will be called Cephas" (which is translated *Peter*).

REFLECT

When Jesus first started to tell people about his mission—to reach out to the people who were hurting, to bring communities back together, to tell people in charge to stop hurting the people they were supposed to be caring for—people were curious about him. They wondered who this new teacher on the scene was.

CONNECT HEAD AND HEART

> **What do you think it would have been like to sit and listen to Jesus for a while?**

> **What do you think it was like for Jesus' followers to give up everything to join in his work?**

> **What are the things you do that you could invite someone to "come and see"?**

They came to check him out and Jesus asked them what they were looking for. And they answered his question with a question (doesn't it bug you when people do that?!): where are you staying? His reply? Come and see.

He didn't try to tell them how important his mission was, not at first. Instead, he invited them to "come and see." It's a simple invitation, but it ends up changing the lives of these people who stay with him that whole day and then end up following him and joining his mission.

Sometimes we think that telling people about who we are or what we believe means we have to do a big speech

He didn't try to tell them how important his mission was, not at first. Instead, he invited them to "come and see." It's a simple invitation, but it ends up changing the lives of these people who stay with him that whole day and then end up following him and joining his mission.

or say a ton on social media or have a lot of answers, when instead it can be as simple as saying "come and see." Come and see what I care about. Come and see what my church is like. Come and see what it's like to be a part of

CONNECT HEART AND HANDS

- Invite one of your friends to "come and see" something that's important to you—and helps other people as well!
- If you don't have anything to invite someone to, maybe the first step is to find a project to get involved in! Is there a community project you could volunteer at? Could you make it a practice to tidy up your neighborhood once a week (or once a month)?

serving food to hungry people or giving away stuff you're not using anymore. Come and see what it's like to be a part of our neighborhood.

Of course, the hard part in inviting people to come and see is that you have to actually be doing something to invite people to! But you can start small. Start where you are. Start putting your faith into practice and then invite others to join you.

JESUS INVITES US TO FEAST

John 6:1–15

READ

After this Jesus went across the Galilee Sea (that is, the Tiberias Sea). A large crowd followed him, because they had seen the miraculous signs he had done among the sick. Jesus went up a mountain and sat there with his disciples. It was nearly time for Passover, the Jewish festival.

Jesus looked up and saw the large crowd coming toward him. He asked Philip, "Where will we buy food to feed these people?" Jesus said this to test him, for he already knew what he was going to do.

Philip replied, "More than a half year's salary worth of food wouldn't be enough for each person to have even a little bit."

One of his disciples, Andrew, Simon Peter's brother, said, "A youth here has five barley loaves and two fish. But what good is that for a crowd like this?"

Jesus said, "Have the people sit down." There was plenty of grass there. They sat down, about five thousand of them. Then Jesus took the bread. When he had given thanks, he distributed it to those who were sitting there. He did the same with the fish, each getting as much as they wanted. When they had plenty to eat, he said to his disciples, "Gather up the leftover pieces, so that nothing will be wasted." So they gathered them and filled twelve baskets with the pieces of the five barley loaves that had been left over by those who had eaten.

When the people saw that he had done a miraculous sign, they said, "This is truly the prophet who is coming into the world." Jesus understood that they were about to come and force him to be their king, so he took refuge again, alone on a mountain.

CONNECT HEAD AND HEART

> What do you think it would have been like to be in the crowd listening to Jesus?

> How would you have felt if you were the young person who had the five loaves and two fish?

> What do you think the disciples learnt from this experience?

> Have you ever worried about having enough food or money? How did that feel? If you haven't had that worry, how do you think it would feel?

> Have you ever felt like you wanted to share something but you were worried that there wasn't enough to go around? What did you do?

> What do you think it would take for everyone in the world to have enough to eat?

REFLECT

As Jesus' ministry and influence grew, people started to seek him out to listen to his teaching. In this particular story they followed him out of the town to a space in the wilderness. When the story tells us he went up a mountain, it was because it was easier to speak to a large crowd if you were a little higher up. Imagine Jesus using the mountain, or hill, as a natural stage. In a time with no electronics or microphones you had to use what was available to you to speak to a crowd.

This story says that in the rule of God everyone will have more than enough. But it also says that it's our responsibility to look out for each other, to share what we have, to make sure no one goes hungry. We live out the rule of God by looking out for each other.

So as Jesus climbs up a little higher than the people, he realizes this crowd has traveled out to see him, away from their homes and community, and that these folks will need to eat, and so he asks one of his inner circle (called the disciples), how are we going to feed these people? The way that the writer of John tells the story, it's as if Jesus already knows what's going to happen. We see this story in several other Gospels and in those Jesus' response to his disciples is different. (Side note: it's interesting and important to pay attention to how storytellers tell the same story differently. What do they emphasize? What do they leave out? What do they change?)

Philip tells Jesus that it would be REALLY expensive to feed all of these people. He's basically saying, "There's no way. They've gotta be on their own!"

Andrew offers that one young person has some food, but it's not going to be enough for everyone.

Now, what happens next has been debated a whole bunch. Some people say that Jesus took the five loaves and two fishes and miraculously multiplied them so that everyone could eat their fill. Other people say that the young person's generosity, of offering their loaves and fishes, encouraged other people to ALSO share what they had brought, and when everyone began to share there was enough for everyone, even those who hadn't been prepared with food of their own.

CONNECT HEART AND HANDS

- **Find some things to donate to a local food bank or another aid organization.**
- **Volunteer at a local organization that helps to feed people who need it.**
- **Explore what resources exist in your town for people who are struggling to have enough food.**

It's important to note something that isn't in the story too. At the time when Jesus was living and ministering, the Roman Empire was in charge and oppressing their community. And in Rome it was the job of the emperor to provide the people with food. Bread and fish were important imports. So for there to be people that were going hungry was a way of the storyteller saying that the emperor wasn't doing his job. When Jesus steps in and gives the people bread and fish, he was doing something the people in power weren't doing. He was meeting needs that other people were failing to meet.

This story says that in the rule of God everyone will have more than enough. But it also says that it's our responsibility to look out for each other, to share what we have, to make sure no one goes hungry. We live out the rule of God by looking out for each other.

This story is an invitation to show up for each other and to make sure that everyone has what they need.

THE MIRACLE OF LAZARUS

John 11:1–44

READ

A certain man, Lazarus, was ill. He was from Bethany, the village of Mary and her sister Martha. (This was the Mary who anointed the Lord with fragrant oil and wiped his feet with her hair. Her brother Lazarus was ill.) So the sisters sent word to Jesus, saying, "Lord, the one whom you love is ill."

When he heard this, Jesus said, "This illness isn't fatal. It's for the glory of God so that God's Son can be glorified through it." Jesus loved Martha, her sister, and Lazarus. When he heard that Lazarus was ill, he stayed where he was. After two days, he said to his disciples, "Let's return to Judea again."

When Jesus arrived, he found that Lazarus had already been in the tomb for four days. Bethany was a little less than two miles from Jerusalem. Many Jews had come to comfort Martha and Mary after their brother's death. When Martha heard that Jesus was coming, she went to meet him, while Mary remained in the house. Martha said to Jesus, "Lord, if you had been here, my brother wouldn't have died. Even now I know that whatever you ask God, God will give you."

Jesus told her, "Your brother will rise again."

CONNECT HEAD AND HEART

> What do you think Jesus' disciples thought of his delay in returning to his friends?

> What do you think Mary and Martha were feeling when they saw Jesus again?

> What do you think it would have been like for Lazarus to experience all of this?

> Have you ever lost someone close to you? How did that make you feel?

> How does it make you feel to think of Jesus crying and being upset at Lazarus' tomb?

> What are some of the things that keep people "bound" and unable to thrive?

Martha replied, "I know that he will rise in the resurrection on the last day."

Jesus said to her, "I am the resurrection and the life. Whoever believes in me will live, even though they die. Everyone who lives and believes in me will never die. Do you believe this?"

She replied, "Yes, Lord, I believe that you are the Christ, God's Son, the one who is coming into the world."

When Mary arrived where Jesus was and saw him, she fell at his feet and said, "Lord, if you had been here, my brother wouldn't have died."

When Jesus saw her crying and the Jews who had come with her crying also, he was deeply disturbed and troubled. He asked, "Where have you laid him?"

They replied, "Lord, come and see."

Jesus began to cry. The Jews said, "See how much he loved him!" But some of them said, "He healed the eyes of the man born blind. Couldn't he have kept Lazarus from dying?"

Jesus was deeply disturbed again when he came to the tomb. It was a cave, and a stone covered the entrance. Jesus said, "Remove the stone."

Martha, the sister of the dead man, said, "Lord, the smell will be awful! He's been dead four days."

Jesus replied, "Didn't I tell you that if you believe, you will see God's glory?" So they removed the stone. Jesus looked up and said, "Father, thank you for hearing me. I know you always hear me. I say this for the benefit of the crowd standing here so that they will believe that you sent me." Having said this, Jesus shouted with a loud voice, "Lazarus, come out!" The dead man came out, his feet bound and his hands tied, and his face covered with a cloth. Jesus said to them, "Untie him and let him go."

His example shows us that we don't have to rush past our hard feelings or our grief. We are invited to sit with those feelings, to feel them, and to express them through our tears and sometimes even our anger. Then we are invited in to the wonder of Lazarus being raised from the dead!

REFLECT

There is a LOT happening in this story from the Gospel of John. We're told that Mary and Martha send word to Jesus that his dear friend Lazarus is sick. I'm sure they were assuming that he would rush to them and heal Lazarus. Jesus, after all, was their close friend and often healed other people. But Jesus decides not to go. At least not right away. He stays put for two days, then tells his disciples that he wants to go to Judea (which is where Bethany was located). This makes his disciples nervous. Bethany was close to Jerusalem, the seat of both political and religious power, and the heat was on for Jesus. His disciples are worried that if they go that close to Jerusalem, Jesus is going to be in danger.

It's important to note that in the Gospel of John, the last of the Gospels to be written, the writer paints the main conflict as between Jesus and the Jewish religious leaders (instead of the Roman political authorities, which is the emphasis of the other Gospel writers). The writer of John's Gospel was writing in a time further removed from the earliest Jesus movement. In this time, the distance (and animosity) between the Jewish religious community and the community of Jewish people who were breaking off to become Christians was growing.

The writer of the Gospel of John probably also wanted to try to stay under the radar of Rome, so if they could make the Jewish people out to be the bad guys (instead of Rome) then it might serve to protect the Jesus followers. It's like how some groups today, both of whom are facing oppression, will fight with each other instead of uniting to fight the people who are oppressing them. It feels safer.

But as we read these stories, far removed from this time and with Christianity as a dominant religion, we have to be careful to make sure anti-Jewish thought and antisemitism don't creep into our theology. The Jewish people are not the enemies of Christians and they were not the reason for Jesus' death.

OK! Back to the story! Even though the disciples are nervous they agree to go with Jesus. Thomas is convinced this will be the end of them and they will die together. Even so, he was willing to go (which says quite a bit about his faith).

They travel to Bethany and find out Lazarus has already died, several days before. Martha comes out to greet Jesus, while Mary refuses to leave the house. You can imagine how sad they were. They were in pain. And they probably felt abandoned by their friend. Mary says as much: "If you had been here, my brother wouldn't have died." Even in the midst of her frustration, she still tells Jesus that she believes he can do something, even now.

Mary joins them and Jesus, now upset and crying too, asks to see where the tomb is. They take him and he asks them to remove the stone. The sisters don't want to; Lazarus has already been in the tomb for several days, the process of decay would have begun. But Jesus insists.

He prays out loud. After he ends his prayer he says, "Lazarus, come out!" And Lazarus walks out of the tomb. But he's still wrapped in the strips of his grave clothes. Wrapped tightly so he can't walk very well. Jesus commands those gathered to untie him and they do.

This is kind of a wild story! One of the things I love about it is the space it gives us to grieve. Even Jesus, who knew the ending, still takes the time to be sad about the loss of his friend. He takes the time to cry over the pain of Mary and Martha. His example shows us that we don't have to rush past our hard feelings or our grief. We are invited to sit with those feelings, to feel them, and to express them through our tears and sometimes even our anger. Then we are invited in to the wonder of Lazarus being raised from the dead! He is restored to the family and community who loved him so much and who were so grieved by his death.

CONNECT HEART AND HANDS

- **If someone you know is grieving or has lost someone recently (or even not so recently) send them a card to let them know you're thinking of them.**
- **Practice sitting with a friend who's having a hard time without offering solutions. Just be with them.**
- **Go back to your list of things that are keeping people bound. Is there something you can do to help to "loose" some of the bindings?**

I also love these final images, of Lazarus coming out of the tomb, and then being helped to get free.

Many of us have had experiences where we've felt trapped by something: by being really sick, by our own decisions, maybe by family situations that aren't that great. It can feel like we need to go it alone, or just rely on God and no one else. This story tells us that we need people around us to help us to get free. We need people around us who can help to untie the bonds that are holding us. God might do the heavy lifting, but we need our community as well.

THEY SHARED EVERYTHING

Acts 2:42–47

READ

The believers devoted themselves to the apostles' teaching, to the community, to their shared meals, and to their prayers. A sense of awe came over everyone. God performed many wonders and signs through the apostles. All the believers were united and shared everything. They would sell pieces of property and possessions and distribute the proceeds to everyone who needed them. Every day, they met together in the temple and ate in their homes. They shared food with gladness and simplicity. They praised God and demonstrated God's goodness to everyone. The Lord added daily to the community those who were being saved.

REFLECT

The book of Acts in the Bible is all about the early Christian movement, as the people who walked with Jesus now invited others to come and see how their lives had been changed as a result. In the very beginning of the movement, just after the resurrection of Jesus, before the people were even calling themselves Christians, before churches were a thing, they were simply groups of people trying to figure out what it meant to be a Jesus follower, what it meant to be a community, and how to continue to spread the teachings and actions of Jesus now that he's gone.

CONNECT HEAD AND HEART

- **What do you think it would be like to live in a community where everyone shared everything they had?**
- **Have you ever had someone give you something you needed? How did you feel?**
- **What different kinds of communities do you belong to? What do you like about each one?**
- **What do you think makes someone want to be a part of the community you're a part of?**
- **When you think about your life of faith, what about it might be compelling to someone else?**

The writer of Acts narrates the story and we see that a couple of things were important to these followers of Jesus. First, listening to the stories of the people who had walked with Jesus (the apostles). In a largely oral culture, this wasn't just about listening to sermons, it was about internalizing the stories of the people who knew Jesus best. People would listen and learn and tell others what they had heard.

Next, the people shared meals together. More than just a picnic, this was also about making sure that everyone had enough to eat. The early Jesus movement incorporated people of all sorts of different economic backgrounds, and one of the priorities was that everyone would have enough. In the family of Jesus, everyone was equal. Which meant that if one person had food and another didn't, it was the Christian duty of the one with food to share with the one who didn't have food.

The writer tells us that sharing even went beyond food: if someone had something and another didn't, the one who had something sold it and gave the money to the one without.

In many ways this was a flattening out of differences. Instead of the rich and the poor, the cool and the nerds, the men and the women, this was an attempt to say that the rules were different in this new community.

In many ways this was a flattening out of differences. Instead of the rich and the poor, the cool and the nerds, the men and the women, this was an attempt to say that the rules were different in this new community.

These new ways of being in community made other people sit up and pay attention. People were watching with interest. And the text tells us this was an effective tool to get other people to join the community: "The Lord added daily to the community those who were being saved." This didn't just mean that people were coming to church on Sunday, it meant that people were shifting how they lived their lives, they were declaring their allegiance to Jesus and to this new way of life, they were saying we want to be a part of this.

CONNECT HEART AND HANDS

- **Think about how you might use what you have to meet the needs of someone else. Can you give someone some clothes? Or sports equipment? Can you offer to share your lunch? Can you sell something and give the money to someone who needs it?**
- **Invite a group of people over for a dinner party and ask each person to bring something to share. Create a dinner with whatever everyone brought.**

It wasn't necessarily people going out and telling people, or trying to convert them, it was living in such a way that people were fascinated and wanted to be a part of it.

People who called themselves Jesus followers lived in such a way that other people were captivated. They were moved, they were inspired, they wanted to be a part of it.

Isn't that a cool vision for the church?

CHANGING THE RULES

Acts 10:9–48

READ

At noon on the following day, as their journey brought them close to the city, Peter went up on the roof to pray. He became hungry and wanted to eat. While others were preparing the meal, he had a visionary experience. He saw heaven opened up and something like a large linen sheet being lowered to the earth by its four corners. Inside the sheet were all kinds of four-legged animals, reptiles, and wild birds. A voice told him, "Get up, Peter! Kill and eat!"

Peter exclaimed, "Absolutely not, Lord! I have never eaten anything impure or unclean."

The voice spoke a second time, "Never consider unclean what God has made pure." This happened three times, then the object was suddenly pulled back into heaven.

Peter was bewildered about the meaning of the vision. Just then, the messengers sent by Cornelius discovered the whereabouts of Simon's house and arrived at the gate. Calling out, they inquired whether the Simon known as Peter was a guest there.

While Peter was brooding over the vision, the Spirit interrupted him, "Look! Three people are looking for you.

Go downstairs. Don't ask questions; just go with them because I have sent them."

So Peter went downstairs and told them, "I'm the one you are looking for. Why have you come?"

They replied, "We've come on behalf of Cornelius, a centurion and righteous man, a God-worshipper who is well-respected by all Jewish people. A holy angel directed him to summon you to his house and to hear what you have to say." Peter invited them into the house as his guests.

CONNECT HEAD AND HEART

> What do you think it would have been like for Peter to have that vision?

> What do you think it would have been like for the followers of Jesus to continue to build the mission and community on their own?

> What do you think about this verse, "I really am learning that God doesn't show any partiality to one group of people over another?" How do you think the world would change if people really believed that?

> Have you ever had an experience that totally changed your mind on something? What was it? How did it make you feel?

The next day he got up and went with them, together with some of the believers from Joppa. They arrived in Caesarea the following day. Anticipating their arrival, Cornelius had gathered his relatives and close friends. As Peter entered the house, Cornelius met him and fell at his feet in order to honor him. But Peter lifted him up, saying, "Get up! Like you, I'm just a human." As they continued to talk, Peter went inside and found a large gathering of people. He said to them, "You all realize that it is forbidden for a Jew to associate or visit with outsiders. However, God has shown me that I should never call a person impure or unclean.

Peter said, "I really am learning that God doesn't show partiality to one group of people over another. Rather, in every nation, whoever worships him and does what is right is acceptable to him. This is the message of peace he sent to the Israelites by proclaiming the good news through Jesus Christ: He is Lord of all! You know what happened throughout Judea, beginning in Galilee after the baptism John preached. You know about Jesus of Nazareth, whom God anointed with the Holy Spirit and endowed with power. Jesus traveled around doing good and healing everyone oppressed by the devil because God was with him. We are witnesses of everything he did, both in Judea and in Jerusalem. They killed him by hanging him on a tree, but God raised him up on the third day and allowed him to be seen, not by everyone but by us. We are witnesses whom God chose beforehand, who ate and drank with him after God raised him from the dead. He commanded us to preach to the people and to testify that he is the one whom God appointed as judge of the living and the dead. All the prophets testify about him that everyone who believes in him receives forgiveness of sins through his name."

While Peter was still speaking, the Holy Spirit fell on everyone who heard the word. The circumcised believers who had come with Peter were astonished that the gift of the Holy Spirit had been poured out even on the Gentiles.

REFLECT

The book of Acts tells the stories of the followers of Jesus trying to continue to spread the word of his mission and life. At the time the story starts, most of the Jesus followers are Jewish. But as the story continues, more and more people from outside the Jewish faith and community are drawn to the message of Jesus and want to join.

This leads to some big questions: Is this new movement open to people who aren't Jewish? If they join, do they have to become Jewish in order to follow Jesus? Do they need to follow all of the same ritual codes and laws as Jewish people?

Underneath all of the questions were even bigger questions: Who is in and who is out? What does it mean for the vision of God to expand beyond a particular place or people or religious group?

Underneath all of the questions were even bigger questions: Who is in and who is out? What does it mean for the vision of God to expand beyond a particular place or people or religious group?

The book of Acts shows how the community of Jesus followers dealt with these questions. Sometimes there were arguments: some people wanted to keep things more exclusive or to make people follow the Jewish rules and laws; other people wanted to change the rules and laws, thereby creating a new movement.

That change would eventually happen with the Jesus movement breaking off and separating from the Jewish faith and forming Christianity.

CONNECT HEART AND HANDS

- **Find someone who has radically changed their mind on something and talk to them about it. (If you can't find someone in person, look for a documentary or book.)**
- **Identify a group of people who get left out at your school or place of worship. What actions could you take to make them feel more welcome?**

But in this early time people's ideas were being challenged and sometimes expanded. In this story, Peter's ideas of who was in and who was out were changed by God. His vision led him to expand his ideas about how big the table was.

This still happens today: we have ideas about who is in and who is out, what kind of people get to sit at the table and which ones don't. And God is continually challenging us to broaden our notions, to stop judging people for what they eat or how they dress or what they believe and welcome them to the table.

The Bible is continually asking us to expand our ideas of what God is doing in the world. It's continually asking us to change our minds, to examine our judgments, and to include even more people.

INTRODUCTION TO THE LETTERS

When it comes to the New Testament, also known as the Christian Scriptures, the bulk of the books are actually letters. In a world before email or video calls, before video streaming and social media, people communicated by writing and sending letters.

In the earliest days of Christianity people gathered for worship in groups that met in people's houses. Sometimes these letters would be addressed to the person who owned the house and to all the people that gathered in their house as part of their community.

These letters were written to help these communities know how to live out their faith. In these early days there weren't Bibles, there weren't devotionals, there weren't people who had gone to seminary and studied and got ordained. There were people who had walked with Jesus, there were other people who had heard the stories of Jesus, and these people shared what they had seen and heard and believed.

When many of the letters were written, the stories of Jesus weren't yet written down; instead they were passed person to person. Many of the letters we have in the Christian Scriptures were written before the Gospels. Many were written by a man named Paul (and still others are credited to Paul even though he probably didn't write them). Paul was trying to help the communities understand what it meant to follow Jesus. Sometimes he was responding to a letter they had written with questions they needed the answers to. Other times he had heard reports of communities who were compromising their values or making concessions and Paul would write to correct their behavior. We don't always have the letters that were written to Paul or the responses to his letters, which means we're often only hearing half of the conversation.

The most important thing to remember as you read any of the letters is they were written to real people, in real places, in a real time. That might seem obvious but it's important because sometimes the advice given in the letters sounds strange to us. Or it advises something that seems counter to how we understand the world. The followers of Jesus then were trying to figure out what it looked like to be a Christian in a world that was often challenging to their beliefs.

These letters are a record of the wrestling. A record of the questions. A record of people working out and forming their theology as they lived their lives.

What did it look like to believe everyone was equal in God's eyes when the world around you elevated some people over others? What did it look like to believe that

God had started a new thing when all around you it seemed like nothing had changed? What did it look like to believe that Jesus was Lord when you lived in a time when saying that out loud would be considered treason? These were not easy questions. People were wrestling with how to live and believe and act.

These letters are a record of the wrestling. A record of the questions. A record of people working out and forming their theology as they lived their lives.

Reading and interpreting these letters responsibly helps us to come and see how they still speak to us today.

BE AN AMBASSADOR

2 Corinthians 5:16–20

READ

So then, from this point on we won't recognize people by human standards. Even though we used to know Christ by human standards, that isn't how we know him now. So then, if anyone is in Christ, that person is part of the new creation. The old things have gone away, and look, new things have arrived!

All of these new things are from God, who reconciled us to himself through Christ and who gave us the ministry of reconciliation. In other words, God was reconciling the world to himself through Christ, by not counting people's sins against them. He has trusted us with this message of reconciliation.

So we are ambassadors who represent Christ. God is negotiating with you through us. We beg you as Christ's representatives, "Be reconciled to God!"

REFLECT

As the early Christians tried to make sense of what their faith meant, there were leaders who tried to help them name what their new community (and therefore what they themselves) should look and act like.

This letter to the church in the city of Corinth is one of those explanations. The writer tries to explain to the Christians how they should think about and treat one another.

CONNECT HEAD AND HEART

> **When you think about what a perfect world looks like, what do you see? How do people behave? What kind of structure is there?**

> **What do you think it looks like to live as if the new age is already here? How would that change your actions?**

> **What does it look like to love and celebrate people who are different from you? (Maybe even people you disagree with?)**

> **What does being an ambassador mean to you? Is that exciting or scary (or something else entirely)?**

In Jewish tradition there was a belief about there being two ages. The old age was an age of sin, death, and violence. It was the age where things were not as they should be. People had power over other people. There was injustice. There were people who didn't have what they needed. They believed that at some point in the future, after the Messiah had come, there would be a NEW age, one that would reflect the rule of God. In this new age there would no longer be violence or death. People would have what they needed. There would be enough.

We live out reconciliation with our words and our actions. We speak to people kindly, even when we disagree. We treat other people with respect. We share what we have. We demonstrate what following the way of Jesus looks like to people who live differently.

The early Christians took this belief of the two ages and built on it, saying that with the life, death, and resurrection of Jesus the new age had begun BUT it wasn't fully here yet. It was as if we got a taste and that taste was enough to inspire us to keep working for the completion of the new age.

So this writer is telling people that in Christ they are part of the new creation. Their new life in the new age has already begun and because of that they needed to treat one another as if they are also part of the new age (because they are).

These early Christians believed that Jesus' death and resurrection caused all things to be reconciled. Reconciliation means that things are made right, brought back into harmony. Divisions are healed, power is equaled, and there isn't any need to fight anymore. Meaning all things, all relationships, all old grudges, and all differences were reconciled, and Christians, who understood that reconciliation and believed in it, were tasked with both living it out AND telling other people about it.

We become "ambassadors" for Christ. An ambassador is someone who represents a country while living in another country. Meaning, someone from the United States, for instance, goes and lives in Ireland to represent the people of the United States to the people of Ireland. A good ambassador is a kind, respected representative of their home country.

CONNECT HEART AND HANDS

- **If you had to give a speech as an ambassador of Jesus, what would you say? Write your speech (and maybe practice giving it to an adult in your life or a friend).**
- **Find something you can do in your community to live out your faith and be an ambassador this week.**

The writer of this passage is calling those who follow in the way of Jesus ambassadors. We are people who go into communities who haven't yet experienced reconciliation and live it out with our words and our example.

This doesn't mean trying to get people to convert to Christianity or to believe in Jesus, it means that we live out reconciliation with our words and our actions. We speak to people kindly, even when we disagree. We treat other people with respect. We share what we have. We demonstrate what following the way of Jesus looks like to people who live differently.

By doing this we show people that another world is possible, a world where people have enough, a world where no one is left out, a world where there is love and kindness, a world where we can respect and admire each other not in spite of our differences but because of them, a world where we work together for peace and for equity.

We get to be ambassadors to show everyone what that dream can look like. Isn't that exciting?

LET'S WORK TOGETHER

Galatians 6:3–10

READ

If anyone thinks they are important when they aren't, they're fooling themselves. Each person should test their own work and be happy with doing a good job and not compare themselves with others. Each person will have to carry their own load.

Those who are taught the word should share all good things with their teacher. Make no mistake, God is not mocked. A person will harvest what they plant. Those who plant only for their own benefit will harvest devastation from their selfishness, but those who plant for the benefit of the Spirit will harvest eternal life from the Spirit. Let's not get tired of doing good, because in time we'll have a harvest if we don't give up. So then, let's work for the good of all whenever we have an opportunity, and especially for those in the household of faith.

REFLECT

Galatians is one of the letters written by Paul. It was written to a new community in faith, one that had probably been brought to faith by Paul. This letter was written before any of the Gospels were written, so this is a community trying to learn what it means to be followers of Jesus and they don't have a lot of the things we have today to rely on. Because Paul didn't stay in one place very long, communities were left on their own. When they had questions, they would have to write a letter, send it to Paul, and wait for a response. They couldn't just ask their pastor because they didn't really have one!

CONNECT HEAD AND HEART

> What do you think it would have been like to be a new Christian without access to a pastor or even a Bible?

> Have you ever compared yourself to someone else?

> Paul says that each person should "test their own work." What do you think he means by that? How do you think you can test your own work?

> Have you ever done something good but for a selfish reason? What was it? How did it make you feel?

> Have you ever done something small but when it was added to work other people did it turned into something a lot bigger?

This new community had started to shift away from the things Paul had told them. Without anyone to rely on, they were being swayed by other communities and religious thinkers around them. Word of their shifting faith made it to Paul somehow and he writes a letter to get them back on track. He's not happy. And he shows it! This letter, of which today's text is the final portion, is often angry, with Paul basically yelling at this community.

He encourages the people in the church in Galatia to not envy other people, to not puff themselves up with arrogance, but instead to look out for each other. To plant a harvest that's not just for their own benefit but for the benefit of others.

Once Paul has corrected the things they were doing wrong and once again reassures them he has valid teaching to offer, he encourages them to be a community of mutual responsibility. Meaning, individuals aren't supposed to just look out for themselves, they're not supposed to be selfish or arrogant; instead they're supposed to work for the good of the community.

He encourages the people in the church in Galatia to not envy other people, to not puff themselves up with arrogance, but instead to look out for each other. To plant a harvest that's not just for their own benefit but for the benefit of others.

In a community where they were closer to the land and to agriculture, these planting examples might mean more to them than they do to us, who, depending on where we live, don't have the same access to gardens or farms. And even those of us who live in more rural areas often still buy the bulk of our food from the grocery store!

But imagine the difference between a private garden in someone's backyard and a community garden where everyone is invited to both help to plant and tend the plants, and to pick the fruit and vegetables when they are ready and share them. In this community garden you might pick and eat something you didn't tend and you might also tend something that someone else gets to eat. But if everyone is working together and doesn't take too much, then everyone will benefit.

CONNECT HEART AND HANDS

- **To understand more about Paul's teaching about planting and harvesting, try your hand at it! Plant a seed (or buy a seedling and tend to it). Notice how much work it takes. Journal about your experience.**
- **If you're in a place where you have a garden or can harvest your own food, make something with what you've harvested and share it with others. How does it change the experience of sharing when you've harvested the ingredients yourself?**
- **If you're not in a place where you can harvest your own food, can you go to a farmer's market or even a grocery store and make something from scratch and then share it?**
- **Find something you can do to be helpful to someone in your family or someone else you know this week.**

This is what it means to plant for the good of others and not just yourself. But it's not just planting; this can also be doing good things around your neighborhood or household (picking up litter or your siblings' toys even if you didn't dump them, things like that). We can do small things that will add up to big things.

If everyone does their part, we'll all be better off.

SOMETIMES WE NEED POETRY

Colossians 1:15–20

READ

The Son is the image of the invisible God,
the one who is first over all creation,
Because all things were created by him:
both in the heavens and on the earth,
the things that are visible and the things that are invisible.
Whether they are thrones or powers,
or rulers or authorities,
all things were created through him and for him.
He existed before all things,
and all things are held together in him.
He is the head of the body, the church,
who is the beginning,
the one who is firstborn from among the dead
so that he might occupy the first place in everything.
Because all the fullness of God was pleased to live in him,
and he reconciled all things to himself through him—
whether things on earth or in the heavens.
He brought peace through the blood of his cross.

REFLECT

Colossians is another of the letters in the Bible. Written to a community that was pretty new to faith, this letter is all about giving them the basics so they can stand firm in the face of people around them who didn't believe the same way they did and wanted them to compromise their values.

The author of this letter, right after they offer their greetings, puts a portion of a song or poem in the letter. These verses might have been something the community used as part of their worship services, or maybe a song they sang when they gathered together.

CONNECT HEAD AND HEART

> **Why do you think the writer of this letter included part of a song or poem?**

> **Have you ever written a song or poem? What did it feel like?**

> **Is there a particular song that makes you feel connected to the Divine? (It can be a song you sing in church, but it doesn't have to be!) Why do you think it moves you the way it does?**

> **Have you ever been criticized because of your faith? What happened?**

> **What does it mean to you that God has the final word?**

It's kind of a complicated poem. Lots of things about existence and who's first and who's at the head. Sometimes people spend a lot of time trying to make this poem into a statement of faith. Something academic and serious.

But the writer could have just laid out a theological statement if that's what he wanted to do. Instead, the writer turns to poetry. There is theology here, for sure, but he's also trying to get at something more than just a statement of faith. He's inviting people into the wonder of the story. Wonder that can only really be captured in poetry or song.

There are certain things that we need to FEEL. We can't just agree to them with our minds. We can't just study them and know them. We need to allow them to be in us, work in us; we need to feel it. And sometimes art helps us do that way better than another argument.

There are certain things that we need to FEEL. We can't just agree to them with our minds. We can't just study them and know them. We need to allow them to be in us, work in us; we need to feel it. And sometimes art helps us do that way better than another argument.

This poem is telling them (and us), this Jesus you're following, who you're getting criticized for following, the one who people are telling you was murdered by the state, the one who people are encouraging you to reject, this Jesus is telling you something about God. Jesus is showing you what God cares about. Jesus is showing you who God is.

CONNECT HEART AND HANDS

- Write a poem or song that expresses what you feel are the most important things about God.
- Find a song that really resonates with you and see if you can track down the story behind it. Why did the writer write it? What does it mean to them?
- Think about something you really want to express to other people. It could be something personal, or about an issue you care about. Can you create a piece of art to help them understand it better?

Jesus and God, in all of this poetic language, are intimately connected. Jesus is the image of God and God, by the way, has created everything and has power over everything. So all of the authorities that are criticizing you, all of the powers that separate you, all of the places where there is injustice, they don't have the final word, God does.

And that is good news.

TEST EVERYTHING

1 Thessalonians 5:21

READ

Test everything, hold fast to that which is good. (NIV)

REFLECT

Sometimes it can feel like our job is to listen to the experts and just believe what they say. We are expected to listen to our parents, listen to our teachers, listen to our pastors, listen to politicians, and so much more. We listen and we follow the rules.

Especially when it comes to faith, it can be easy to believe the things that we're told. Depending on what kind of religious tradition we come from, we can feel like we're not allowed to ask questions or have doubts or push back.

I love this verse from 1 Thessalonians. It's an instruction that whatever we're taught, in whatever context, we should test it. Ask questions. Try it out. Talk to other people. See how this thing works for them. And then, if it does work, if we experience it to be true, if we see it works for other people, if we experience its goodness, then we hold on to it.

CONNECT HEAD AND HEART

> What advice have you received that you realized really worked?
> Have you ever received advice that wasn't good? What happened?
> When someone tells you something, how do you decide whether to believe them or not?
> How does this verse help you think differently about your faith?

This idea of testing everything isn't about being hardheaded or refusing to listen to others, it's about taking responsibility for your own life, faith, and behavior. Instead of just doing what other people tell us, this verse asks us to consider our own experiences, wisdom, and way of being. We need to be responsible for the things we do instead of just saying, "Well, I was just following what other people told me!"

Ask questions. Try it out. Talk to other people. See how this thing works for them. And then, if it does work, if we experience it to be true, if we see it works for other people, if we experience its goodness, then we hold on to it.

At the same time, this verse asks us to really listen to other people, to take feedback without being defensive, to listen to people who know more than us, and to use all of their wisdom to make good decisions.

This can be a balancing act sometimes. Many of us tend to veer too far one way or the other: just doing what everyone else says OR refusing to listen to anyone at all. In order to make the best decisions we can, we need to both trust our own experiences and desires AND trust people who have more experience than we do.

CONNECT HEART AND HANDS

- **Take a piece of advice you've been given and test some experiments to see how you can tell if it's good advice or not.**
- **Ask some adults in your life how they weigh what advice to take and what advice to ignore.**
- **Ask some adults in your life to tell you a story of when they ignored some advice they should have taken and taken advice they should have ignored.**

We can also use this verse when someone is telling us something about God or the church. As we listen to what they are saying, we can weigh it and test it: Does this belief cause harm to people? Does this belief feel in line with God's stated care for the most vulnerable? Does this teaching uphold or diminish the full humanity of people? By asking these questions we can figure out if something is in line with the good news of God or if it's something that is harmful or a distortion.

POWER TO THE YOUTH

1 Timothy 4:11–16

READ

Command these things. Teach them. Don't let anyone look down on you because you are young. Instead, set an example for the believers through your speech, behavior, love, faith, and by being sexually pure. Until I arrive, pay attention to public reading, preaching, and teaching. Don't neglect the spiritual gift in you that was given through prophecy when the elders laid hands on you. Practice these things, and live by them so that your progress will be visible to all. Focus on working on your own development and on what you teach. If you do this, you will save yourself and those who hear you.

REFLECT

The book of 1 Timothy is another letter. Scholars think this is one that wasn't actually written by Paul but was instead written in his name and addressed to Timothy. Timothy had converted to Christianity, traveled with Paul, and then became a representative of Paul, traveling on his own to churches and pastoring at least one. This letter is written to Timothy, encouraging him in his faith and ministry.

In a lot of ways, we're eavesdropping on a conversation between two specific people, but that doesn't mean the advice given in the letter only applies to Timothy. It's like when you overhear a friend giving another friend advice on a certain situation and you realize it applies to you too. I especially appreciate these words given to someone who was maybe quite a bit younger than the people surrounding them (because I feel like many of us have had the experience of being the youngest in the room and therefore feeling overlooked)!

CONNECT HEAD AND HEART

> **Have you ever felt like people were looking down on you or dismissing you because of your age? What did they do? What did it feel like?**

> **Are there things you think you could help older people in your life understand BECAUSE of your age? What are they?**

> **What do you think of the idea of being able to be an example to people who are older than you?**

> **Are there certain areas of your behavior, speech, love, or faith where you need to develop yourself more? What are those areas? What are some things you might need to do or try?**

The author's advice to Timothy is given specifically to someone who was in leadership. He might have been being ignored or having a hard time asserting his authority because of his age. The writer reminds him that he has gifts, and not only that, but because the elders laid hands on him (this could be similar to what happens at an ordination or commissioning) he DOES have authority to lead. The way to gain respect is to stand firm in his calling and to set an example with his behavior.

Even as young people we have the opportunity to lead in our communities on things that are important to us. We just have to lead by example.

By leading the way with actions, he'll show others how to live as well. The final bit of advice is to focus on your own development. Sometimes when we feel like we're being ignored or overlooked we can counter that by protesting that we ARE ready, we ARE smart, we ARE leaders. That sometimes has the opposite effect on those who are looking down on us; it affirms that we're not ready. But if we focus on our actions, doing what we know needs to be done, working to improve in areas where we are weaker, people will see our commitment and our work and know that we're ready.

One thing to note: the writer of this letter talks about "being sexually pure" and some people have used that over the years to shame women, to alienate or condemn LGBTQ+ folks, or to put in place rigid ideas around purity.

I think it's important to remember that this was advice to someone who was in leadership and therefore has different standards around behavior. This advice could be reminding Timothy to be ethical in his relationships, to not use his power to benefit sexually from others, to not be involved in some of the cultic practices of his day that included sexual behavior, to make sure that whatever he was doing sexually was honest and filled with integrity. And that is still good advice for us today: to make sure that we're living in line with our own values and ethics, to make sure our relationships are healthy and consensual, and to make sure we're not using sexuality to manipulate, denigrate, shame, or hurt others.

CONNECT HEART AND HANDS

- **Using the list you made above, make a plan to tackle one of the areas you identified wanting to grow in.**
- **Pick an area or an issue where you feel called to be a leader. Do some research to find out all you can about that issue.**
- **Think about ways you can set an example with your behavior, speech, love, and faith. Then work on doing it!**

Even as young people we have the opportunity to lead in our communities on things that are important to us. We just have to lead by example.

YOU CAN'T DO IT ALONE

Hebrews 10:22–25

READ

Therefore, let's draw near with a genuine heart with the certainty that our faith gives us, since our hearts are sprinkled clean from an evil conscience and our bodies are washed with pure water.

Let's hold on to the confession of our hope without wavering, because the one who made the promises is reliable.

And let us consider each other carefully for the purpose of sparking love and good deeds. Don't stop meeting together with other believers, which some people have gotten into the habit of doing. Instead, encourage each other, especially as you see the day drawing near.

REFLECT

Hebrews is another letter, written to a community to encourage them in their faith. The section we read today is all about community. The writer of this letter encourages people to draw near to one another and to God because they are secure and certain in their faith. They are also encouraged to hold on to hope, believing that the promises they've received from God are reliable. And finally, they are encouraged to continue to meet together with other people of faith.

CONNECT HEAD AND HEART

> What does hope mean to you? What are some things that give you hope?

> What do you think of the phrase "sparking love and good deeds"? How do people encourage love and good deeds in you? How might you encourage the same in others?

> Do you have friends who are people of faith? What is it like when you get together?

> Do you talk about your faith with other people (not to convert them, just to share what you're thinking about)? Why or why not?

> Think of a time when someone did something that was really encouraging to you. What was it? What happened? How did it make you feel?

A lot of people read this passage and think it means making sure that you go to church, but I think the writer is talking about more than that. The writer is saying that faith is best done in community. When we meet together with other people of faith we can encourage one another to have hope, to be certain in our faith, and to continue to love other people and do good deeds.

Sometimes when we're on our own it can be easy to have our faith waver, or to struggle to have hope. We can get stuck in our heads or focused on the things in our lives that aren't going like we want them to. Being around other people who believe in a similar way as we do, people who share the same values, people who are working toward the same goals, helps us to see that there is more going on than just our experience. Other people can remind us of good things that are happening, they can remind us that we are loved, they can remind us that we are not alone.

Living out our faith is a communal thing. We need other people to help us learn, grow, and reflect. And we need to encourage others as well.

We, too, have a responsibility to encourage others. To remind THEM they are loved, to remind them that good things are happening.

Together we can cheer one another on as we spread love in the world and do good deeds. And the deeds we

CONNECT HEART AND HANDS

- Make a list of things that give you hope. They can be big things or little things. Put the list somewhere you will see it often and read it at least every couple of days.
- Do something with other people of faith. Maybe go and serve a meal somewhere, or talk about your favorite Bible stories, or go to a worship service together.

do together will have more of an impact than just the things we do alone.

Living out our faith is a communal thing. We need other people to help us learn, grow, and reflect. And we need to encourage others as well.

So find your people. Work together to put more love and justice into the world. Encourage each other to have hope and faith. We're in this together!

MORE THAN JUST WORDS

James 1:19–27

READ

Know this, my dear brothers and sisters: everyone should be quick to listen, slow to speak, and slow to grow angry. This is because an angry person doesn't produce God's righteousness. Therefore, with humility, set aside all moral filth and the growth of wickedness, and welcome the word planted deep inside you—the very word that is able to save you.

CONNECT HEAD AND HEART

> What are some things that make you angry?

> Have you ever done something when you were angry that you later regretted? What happened?

> How do you keep yourself from acting out your anger?

> Do you think there is ever an anger that is a good thing?

You must be doers of the word and not only hearers who mislead themselves. Those who hear but don't do the word are like those who look at their faces in a mirror. They look at themselves, walk away, and immediately forget what they were like. But there are those who study the perfect law, the law of freedom, and continue to do it. They don't listen and then forget, but they put it into practice in their lives. They will be blessed in whatever they do.

The early church paid special attention to people who were vulnerable and didn't have protectors. We are encouraged to do the same today.

If those who claim devotion to God don't control what they say, they mislead themselves. Their devotion is worthless. True devotion, the kind that is pure and faultless before God the Father, is this: to care for orphans and widows in their difficulties and to keep the world from contaminating us.

REFLECT

This passage from the book of James is all about words and actions. The writer first encourages people to pay attention to how they use their words in community, to listen more than they speak, and to be slow to anger.

Next, the writer talks about people who listen but don't act. This could be something like knowing the right thing to do and choosing not to do it. Or listening to your parent or guardian tell you something, saying you'll do it, and then not doing it. Or to think about helping someone out and not following through. The writer is saying it's important to put our faith, our values, what we believe, into action. We need to not just speak but also do.

And then the writer offers some specific examples: to care for orphans and widows, and to make sure the world doesn't contaminate us.

This section might seem a little confusing, so let's unpack it. Caring for orphans and widows was about taking care of people who were vulnerable. In the time when this author was writing, if you were a child who didn't have adults to care for you, you were left out on your own. There weren't the same kind of systems we have in place today to move children into some other form of care. Same thing for widows: if you were a woman without a man to protect you, you were at risk. It would be hard to take care of yourself. The early church paid special attention to people who were vulnerable and didn't have protectors. We are encouraged to do the same today.

The writer is also encouraging the listeners "to keep the world from contaminating us." Some people over the years have used this passage to say that Christians shouldn't do worldly things like watch certain movies, or dress in a certain way, or listen to certain types of music. Instead, Christians should be set apart because the "world" is dirty and bad. But other pastors and scholars look at this passage differently. It's not that things in the world are necessarily bad or dirty, it's that they can distract us from doing all of the other things this passage tells us God wants us to do.

CONNECT HEART AND HANDS

- Think of some ways to calm yourself down before speaking when you get angry. Next time you get mad about something, practice your calming techniques first.
- Find an organization in your area that cares for kids who don't have (or are separated from) their parents and see what you can do to help out.
- If you belong to a church where there are older folks who might be lonely, send one of them a card, bring them some goodies, or find a way to connect and encourage them.

If we look at certain types of media, and even people who are in control, it might be easy to have our anger feel justified. Or to think it's OK to say hurtful things. We can forget that we're supposed to care about people who are vulnerable. We might start to think we should just look out for ourselves and not worry about people we don't know. We can start to think the values of some parts of society—to take what you want, to not care about creation, to get as much money as you can, to disregard the feelings of others—are the values we should hold. This writer is saying, stay focused on the values of God. Pay attention to living out your faith as you move through the world.

It can be hard sometimes, but centering kindness, being a good listener, putting our faith into action, and looking out for the vulnerable leads to stronger communities—and that's a beautiful thing.

SHOW YOUR LOVE

1 John 3:16–18

READ

This is how we know love: Jesus laid down his life for us, and we ought to lay down our lives for our brothers and sisters. But if someone has material possessions and sees a brother or sister in need but refuses to help—how can the love of God dwell in a person like that?

CONNECT HEAD AND HEART

- > Why do you think the writer of this letter wants the community to love each other with actions?
- > Have you ever had an experience where someone SAID they loved you but their actions said something different? What happened? How did that feel?
- > What are some things other people do that make you feel really loved?
- > What are some of the ways you can love the people in your life with your actions?

Little children, let's not love with words or speech but with action and truth.

REFLECT

Sometimes, despite scholars' best investigations, it's hard to know all of the things about certain books of the Bible. The book of 1 John is one of those. Often considered a letter, it's missing some of the elements of a letter (a greeting and a sign off). We're also not entirely sure who wrote it, when it was written, or where it was written. But even without those details we do know that it was, indeed, written and it was written by a particular person in a specific place to another community of people to help them live out their faith.

The writer of the letter is telling them words aren't enough. You have to actually follow through and act.

It might have originally been a sermon, or a letter, or some other type of message that was passed around. It was written years after Jesus' death as communities were growing and figuring out what it meant to follow Jesus.

The writer of 1 John wants to challenge the people receiving this letter on the places where they're falling short and encourage them to live up to the example of Jesus.

In the section we read today, the writer reminds the community that the love of Jesus was about action. Jesus was willing to do whatever it took to love his people, even facing death! The community is being encouraged to commit to the way of Jesus: to commit to loving other people, commit to providing and caring for them, commit to doing whatever is needed to make sure they experience liberation.

CONNECT HEART AND HANDS

- **Go back to the list you made of how you can show love with your actions. Choose one of the ways and do it this week.**
- **This week, if someone asks you for something that you can do for them, do it! Then reflect about how it felt.**

It seems that in this particular community there were some people who were talking a good game: they were saying they loved other people, but they weren't doing anything to help them. They were saying they loved people who were poor or hungry, but they didn't do anything to feed or clothe them. The writer of the letter is telling them words aren't enough. You have to actually follow through and act.

It's not enough to say you're following Jesus, to say you love someone, to say you're a Christian, if your behavior doesn't match. This isn't about trying to be perfect, or always getting it right, but it is about striving to match your actions to your beliefs.

It's easy to say that you love someone or that you care about a particular group of people or a cause. But what are you doing to support those people or that cause? Are you willing to support them even when it's inconvenient? Or when it might cost you something? That's the true test.

Our faith isn't just about what we believe. It's not just about having the right ideas. It's about how those beliefs and ideas impact our behavior.

You can't just say you love someone, you have to show them.

A PERFECT CITY

Revelation 21:1–7

READ

Then I saw a new heaven and a new earth, for the former heaven and the former earth had passed away, and the sea was no more. I saw the holy city, New Jerusalem, coming down out of heaven from God, made ready as a bride beautifully dressed for her husband. I heard a loud voice from the throne say, "Look! God's dwelling is here with humankind. He will dwell with them, and they will be his peoples. God himself will be with them as their God. He will wipe away every tear from their eyes. Death will be no more. There will be no mourning, crying, or pain anymore, for the former things have passed away." Then the one seated on the throne said, "Look! I'm making all things new." He also said, "Write this down, for these words are trustworthy and true." Then he said to me, "All is done. I am the Alpha and the Omega, the beginning and the end. To the thirsty I will freely give water from the life-giving spring. Those who emerge victorious will inherit these things. I will be their God, and they will be my sons and daughters.

REFLECT

Sometimes people think about the book of Revelation as a scary book. It's filled with visions and violent imagery. Some folks use it as a fortune-telling piece, saying it spells out how the end of the world is going to go down. Many people in more progressive churches kind of ignore the book, or don't really know what to do with it. It's definitely a complicated one!

CONNECT HEAD AND HEART

> **What have you been taught (if anything) about the book of Revelation?**
>
> **What do you think this vision of a new Jerusalem would have meant to the people who were hearing this for the first time?**
>
> **If you were creating a new city, a perfect city, what would it look like? Feel like? Sound like?**

The book of Revelation is part letter and part storytelling. It was written in a time when there was increasing oppression of the new Christian community. John, the author of the letter, has been sent to the island of Patmos to be in exile. While there he writes this book and uses the language of visions to tell the story.

A lot of scholars agree that John is using coded language, not to tell the future but to describe the present state of things. He's making up fantastic beasts but talking about them in a way that insiders would know who he's referring to: real people, real political leaders, who are at that moment doing harm to the most vulnerable in their communities.

The visions John paints ARE violent and it can be hard to grapple with that. We need to remember that this was written to a community that didn't have the strength or power to fight back in that way. These violent ideas are the fantasies of the oppressed. Does that make them right? Not necessarily, but it does make them more understandable.

All of the warnings and violence lead up to these final chapters that paint a much different picture. These final images tell us of a new heaven and earth, a new Jerusalem (the center of hope for the Jewish people), and a God who dwells, in person, with God's people. It's a vision of peace and hope. It's a vision where grief, pain, and tears will be no more.

It's a vision of hope for a people who were struggling to have hope.

In a world that is sometimes scary, where it can feel like we don't have a lot of power, where so many things are

This vision is also an invitation to us to continue to not only come and see the dream of the new heaven and new earth but to work for it as well.

CONNECT HEART AND HANDS

- **Take what you wrote about the new, perfect city, and draw a map of it.**
- **What's one thing you could do where you currently live to bring it a little closer to the perfect city you've envisioned? Do that this week!**

hard and sad, this promise of God dwelling with us and making everything OK is one we can hang on to.

This vision is also an invitation to us to continue to not only come and see the dream of the new heaven and new earth but to work for it as well.

WHAT'S NEXT?

Now that you've finished this book you might be wondering where to turn next! How do you continue to come and see (and invite others to come and see) the power of faith and justice working in the world? Here are some ideas:

> Invite a friend to read this book with you and go through it again!
> Revisit some of the entries that spoke to you the most.
> Make a plan to do some of the heart and hands adventures that you didn't have time for the first time through.
> Read the book again, making a note of how your answers, thoughts, and ideas are changing or what new things are sticking out to you.
> Pick one of the books of the Bible and read the whole thing, making a note of questions as you go.
> Choose one thing in your faith to learn more about.

Our faith is something that continues to grow and change as we continue to grow and change. The invitation to come and see isn't a one-time thing, it's an ongoing invitation into a life of more depth, more wholeness, and more justice.

Even though this book is over, your journey has just begun!

ABOUT THE AUTHOR

Shannon TL Kearns is a priest, a playwright, and an author. He loves telling stories of all kinds because he believes stories help us see ourselves and each other better.

Shannon has worked in lots of different types of churches, as the artistic director of a theatre company, as a workshop teacher, and lots of other random jobs over the years as well. His passion is writing and preaching and creating communities that care about working for justice together.

In his spare time he's a fan of reading books (he tries to read 100 a year!), putting together LEGO sets, and cooking.

He lives with his wife, Ashley, and their two cats and a dog in Kansas.